Taranto

The Raid, The Observer, The Aftermath

*To: Ian, Kellen, & Abe —
All the best!
Christopher O'Connor*

Christopher O'Connor

Photo Credits

The photograph of the Fairey Swordfish appears by permission of the Imperial War Museum. The entire IWM collection, including photos, film, and sound recordings, can be found at www.iwmcollections.org.uk.

The photograph of HMS Illustrious appears by permission of the Australian War Memorial. The AWM collection can be found at www.awm.gov.au.

The photograph of Opie's passport picture was taken by the author. The passport had been loaned to the author by Opie's son, Fitzhugh Lee Rhea Opie.

The maps were designed by the author and produced by Debra Greer of Main Street Grafix, Independence, VA.

© 2010 Christopher O'Connor
All Rights Reserved.

No part of this publication may be reproduced, stored in a retrieval system, or transmitted, in any form or by any means, electronic, mechanical, photocopying, recording, or otherwise, without the written permission of the author.

First published by Dog Ear Publishing
4010 W. 86th Street, Ste H
Indianapolis, IN 46268
www.dogearpublishing.net

dog ear
PUBLISHING

ISBN: 978-160844-721-3

This book is printed on acid-free paper.

Printed in the United States of America

For Paul,
who got away from us far too soon

INTRODUCTION

On November 11, 1940 - more than a year before the attack on Pearl Harbor - aircraft of the Royal Navy executed a surprise attack on the capital ships of the Italian Navy at their home port of Taranto. The attack was a rousing success: three battleships were severely damaged, needing months of repair work. The battleship strength of the Italian Fleet was cut in half. Attacking the enemy's ships while they were anchored was not a new idea: Admiral Horatio Nelson had famously done so at the Nile (1798) and Copenhagen (1803)[1]. However, the use of aircraft in such a mission was a new idea: using the power of carrier-launched aircraft to dramatically increase the range of naval power. The Taranto attack was launched from a point 170 miles away from the target. This increase in range meant that the only way for potential targets to protect themselves during the coming five years of war would be to actively search with their own aircraft (or radar) for the approaching attacker. All the navies of the world would study the Taranto attack, but few would learn this most important of the many lessons of the British success on that November night. To its everlasting sorrow and shame, the United States Navy did not learn that lesson until December 7, 1941.

It is instructive to compare the Taranto and Pearl Harbor attacks. In each case, carrier-based aircraft used torpedoes to inflict severe damage on battleships thought to be ensconced in safe harbors. Both attacking forces achieved surprise, the Japanese more so than the British. Both attackers modified their weapons for the specific conditions of the chosen target: by modifying torpedoes to allow them to be used successfully in water previously thought to have been too shallow. The defenders in each case fell victim to a "it can't happen here" mentality which weakened the arguments of those who called for better preparedness. Local commanders at Taranto and Pearl Harbor were restricted by the actions and decisions of political and military leaders in Rome and Washington. Both attackers put many ships at sea in the days prior to the attack, and these multiple ship movements confused the defenders as to the true destination and target. Each attack was made in two slightly separated waves, reinforcing the damage and shock of the first attack with a second one, and allowing the selection of alternate targets based on early success. The Admirals in command of the attacking forces each considered remaining in the area to deliver further blows, but after seeing the great success and the small price paid for it, retired from the battle content with the results achieved.

The magnitude of the Royal Navy's accomplishment is demonstrated by comparing their equipment to that deployed by the Japanese a year later. The British deployed one carrier; Admiral Nagumo commanded a task force of six. Twenty-one aircraft flew off *HMS Illustrious* for the strike at Taranto; the Japanese sent 355 planes over Hawaii. The Japanese flew Zeroes, Kates, and Vals: all-metal monoplanes with speeds of 200 - 300 mph, while the British pilots flew the Fairey Swordfish, a fabric-covered biplane with a top speed of 140 mph. In addition, the British attacked at night, complicating their navigation and targeting. No other navy in the world was capable of nighttime carrier operation in 1940. The British are justifiably proud of the victory won by those twenty pilots and the hundreds of sailors, mechanics, and officers who supported them. Taranto Night is to this day celebrated in the Royal Navy.

The attack on Taranto announced in a violent and abrupt way that the long inter-war argument among naval officers was over: the aircraft carrier would be the dominant naval weapon of World War II, not the battleship. Neutral navies might be expected to move more slowly than those of combatant countries to adapt to the changes and improvements in weaponry and tactics that come with combat. Still, a professional officer corps is charged with just that responsibility: to study and learn from the combat experience of other nations. That the US Navy did a poor job of analyzing and applying the lessons of the Taranto attack is made more remarkable by a little known fact: an officer in the US Navy was aboard *HMS Illustrious* for the entire attack cruise, and reported in detail to Washington on all aspects of the attack.

He was Lt. Commander John N. Opie, III and his story is fascinating. An Annapolis graduate (Class of 1924), he was plucked suddenly in May 1940 from an otherwise unremarkable navy career, and sent to England after only 3 days of orientation and training. From July 1940 until March 1941 he sailed into combat on a wide variety of British warships. His actions as an observer violated the Neutrality Acts, and at least once drew complaints from

State Department personnel[2]. He wrote dozens of reports on his observations, many of which were widely distributed through the US Navy. On his return to the US in April 1941 he had more combat experience than any officer in the Navy. Yet he did no more intelligence work, and was not used in any way that would capitalize on his unique experience. After four months of desk work in Washington, he was given command of a destroyer in the Atlantic Fleet. On December 7, 1941, he was with his ship, *USS Roe*, anchored at Halvjafjord, Iceland, awaiting another convoy protection mission.

This book has three objectives: to describe the Taranto attack and its immediate consequences, to tell Opie's story in detail, and to consider the aftermath of the Taranto attack from the perspectives of the major naval powers. There are lessons in these three tales that are relevant today: lessons regarding surprise attack and the ability of intelligence work to anticipate and prevent it.

THE RAID

Planning and Training

The attack on Taranto was the result of long and careful planning by the Royal Navy. Still, the British had to adapt to circumstances in the summer and fall of 1940 that were not foreseen during the late thirties when plans first drawn up. The success of the attack indicates that they accomplished both tasks.

War came to the Mediterranean on June 10, 1940, the day that Mussolini declared war on France and Great Britain. However, the threat of war had been high on at least three occasions in the prior decade: in 1935, when Italy attacked Ethiopia despite the opposition of Britain, France, and the League of Nations; in 1938, when Germany annexed Austria; and in 1939 when Hitler threatened Czechoslovakia prior to the settlement at Munich. On each of these occasions, Royal Navy officers considered potential naval actions in the Mediterranean. The plans that resulted always advocated an early strike on Italian Fleet units at anchor. A number of RN officers had served with the Italians during WWI, and these men were familiar with Italian ports and ships. This familiarity led them to believe that a surprise attack made immediately upon the opening of hostilities would catch the Italian Fleet unprepared. Such a plan was first worked up aboard *HMS Glorious* during the Ethiopian crisis in 1935[1]. *Glorious* was an aircraft carrier built on the hull of a poorly designed battle cruiser from WWI. She displaced 22,500 tons, carried 35 aircraft, and was capable of 31 knots. When she joined the fleet in 1930, she represented the latest thinking in design of aircraft carriers. In the late thirties, she was a floating academy of naval aviation for the British. During these years, the Fleet Air Arm developed its tactics and operating principles. The pilots aboard *Glorious* tested high-level bombing and dive bombing, but rejected both — the first as inaccurate, and the second as too risky for the pilots. The fliers concentrated on torpedo bombing, and became highly skilled in this tactic.[2] Dropping a torpedo from an airplane requires the pilot to fly as close to the water and as slowly as possible. The Swordfish was the perfect aircraft for this mission, being incapable of flying very fast or very high. British commanders initially favored dawn and dusk attacks, because the enemy ships would be silhouetted, and the attacking planes hidden, by sunrise or sunset. They changed this doctrine after testing it in the Mediterranean, however. They found that the sun rises and sets very quickly in the Med, making it difficult to arrive precisely at the right time. Instead, they began working on nighttime attacks. This made them unique among the navies of the world: as no one else even flew after dark. Years of training made the FAA pilots expert at launching, navigating, and returning to the carrier in the black of night. During night attacks, the FAA would drop flares behind the target ships, and attack these ships illuminated by the magnesium flares. In late 1939, *HMS Glo-*

rious was withdrawn from the Mediterranean. Her aircrews were broken up; many of the pilots being reassigned to new carriers soon to be launched.

As Britain made plans for a potential naval war in the Mediterranean, it was assumed that the French Fleet would fight as an ally of England's. Accordingly, pre-war plans assigned the RN primary responsibility for the Eastern Med, using British bases on Malta and in Egypt. The French would patrol the Western end of the Med from their bases at Toulon and in North Africa. The Fall of France in May 1940 consigned these plans to the rubbish basket. While the ships of the French navy remained scattered around various ports, the Vichy government negotiated with a triumphant Germany, hoping to keep control of that navy and thereby, keep those ships neutral. Churchill worried about the Germans taking these ships, and greatly bolstering their small navy. During June, the British tried to convince the French to place the ships of their navy in a safe place: either in British controlled ports or in the French Carribean port of Martinique. The French rejected these ideas, intending to hold on to the fleet, but also to deny it to the Germans. On July 3, 1940, the British demanded the surrender of French ships at Alexandria, Oran, and in several English ports. At Alexandria, the French gave in to the gentle persuasion of Admiral Cunningham; and at the British ports the ships were taken, some of them by force. Most important, at Oran on July 3, 1940, Admiral Gensoul, the French commander, refused to discuss any accommodation of British demands; and the Royal Navy force under Admiral Somerville opened fire on the French ships at anchor. Two were sunk, others damaged, and nearly 1000 French sailors were killed. Several ships escaped the harbor and made it to Toulon. The result was that the French Navy maintained an enduring hostility to Britain; and that the British fought this Mediterranean naval war alone[3].

Their opponent would be the *Regia Marina*; Mussolini's chosen instrument for dominating the *Mare Nostrum*. As the war began, Italy's strategic goal was to dominate the sea lanes in order to do two things: run supplies and troops to North Africa, and deny the British access to Egypt and India. Britain would fight to maintain the Mediterranean route to her colonial empire; and to control the sea in order to attack military, economic and other targets in Italy. A preview of the battle to come will review strengths and weaknesses of the two contending sides.

Bases, Ships & Planes

The British held strong - but scattered - positions in the Mediterranean. Their bases at Malta, Gibraltar, and Alexandria were large and well-defended. The primary base for the RN was Malta, the island in the central Mediterranean, equidistant (1100 miles) from Gibraltar and Alexandria. The British had invested a fortune in building up the facilities at Malta, but many RN officers felt that its proximity to the Italian mainland meant that it could not be defended. During the thirties, the British waffled over Malta, sometimes reinforcing it and other times denying it the additional weapons and facilities it needed. The Army and the RAF felt that Malta could not be defended, especially against Italian air power. In the end, the Navy insisted on maintaining Malta, evacuating civilians in July 1940; and stripping the base down to its essential requirements. Malta's closeness to Italy gave it value as a base for potential offensive action, and for intelligence gathering as well. Its docks and repair facilities would be useful, even if most ships would only anchor there for short periods of time. However, limited budgets prevented the Royal Navy from properly outfitting Malta for these tasks. By the fall of 1940, it was poorly prepared for war, especially as it had almost no air defense — neither planes nor AA guns in anywhere near adequate numbers. Accordingly, Alexandria and Gibraltar were stocked with food, fuel, and ammunition in the expectation that they would carry a greater burden of supporting the Fleet. Facilities such as airfields, fuel depots, and living quarters were added or improved. There was also a British base on Cyprus, in the far Eastern Mediterranean; and from 31 October 1940, Britain gained access to Crete, especially the port at Suva Bay.

Italy's great base was, of course, the Italian peninsula itself, jutting into the Central Mediterranean like a giant boot. Mussolini famously claimed that Italy had no need for aircraft carriers, since Italy herself was a natural air base. The islands of Sardinia and Sicily gave further opportunity to monitor and control the sea lanes. The small island of Pantelleria sat midway in the 90-mile channel that ran between Tunisia's Cape Bon and Sicily's port of Marsala. Italy's North African colony of Lybia lay roughly 500 miles away; offering a large base at Tripoli and a smaller on at Benghazi. Italy also had small air bases on Rhodes and Leros in the Eastern Mediterranean. Naples was a substantial port, and well situated to project Italian power into the western Mediterranean. At Taranto, the Italians had taken a fine natural harbor and turned it into a major naval asset. They built breakwaters extending from the north and south edges of the harbor to the island of San Pietro, thereby creating a large circular anchorage known as the Mar Grande. To the northeast, accessible by a canal, was a smaller anchorage called the Mar Piccolo. Viewing the harbor as a clock face, the city of Taranto lay between the two lagoons, from the 12 to the 2 o'clock position. An oil storage depot was located to the southeast, at five o'clock. A pipeline led from this depot to the Mar Grande, allowing ships to refuel. A seaplane base, with large hangars, occupied the shore of the Mar Piccolo to the northeast of the main anchorage. Shops and docks crowded the edges of both anchorages. Anti-aircraft batteries were located around the entire circumference of the Mar Grande, and barrage balloons would be tied down to some thirty locations. The Italians placed great hope in sound detection equipment that would "hear" the noise from the engines of attacking aircraft. Steel nets that would protect ships at anchor from torpedo attack were being laid down in the fall of 1940, but would not be completed before the Royal Navy attacked.

As the fighting developed, Alexandria became the primary British naval base in the Mediterranean. The Fleet based there—commanded by Vice Admiral Andrew Browne Cunningham—generally deployed one carrier, two or three battleships, nine or ten light cruisers, thirty destroyers, and a dozen submarines. The ships tended to be older and slower than the best vessels in the RN, but still constituted a potent naval force. At the outset, the carrier was *HMS Eagle*. Commissioned in 1924, she was old and slow. Built on the hull of an abandoned battle-cruiser, she was capable of only 24 knots. She carried only 30 aircraft. At Gibraltar, a smaller force, which from 1940 came to be known as "Force H"; usually counted among its assets a battleship or two, half a dozen cruisers, and 15 destroyers. As new carriers joined the fleet, Force H gained a carrier of its own after 1940.

The Italian Navy experienced a considerable build up during the thirties. Italian ships - of all classes - were built for speed, and they delivered. In 1940, they deployed six battleships, seven heavy and 12 light cruisers, 50 destroyers, and 100 submarines. Two of the battleships were brand new; with 15" main guns and speeds of 32 knots. The other four were WWI vessels extensively rebuilt in the 1930's. The cruisers and destroyers were well armed and much faster than their British counterparts. The numerous subs were mechanically frail and very noisy, but the Italians had some outstanding light units: patrol boats, frogmen, and human-controlled mines which were well-trained and turned out to be highly effective. They never did launch an aircraft carrier, though one was under construction when Italy surrendered in 1943. More important, the Italian Navy never developed a *naval* air arm, aside from a few cruiser-launched sea planes. This meant that long range reconnaissance was conducted by Air Force pilots in Air Force planes. These pilots were not well trained in ship recognition, naval formations, or estimation of speed. Throughout the war, the Italian Navy would suffer from poor information about the British navy's position, speed, composition, and course[4].

The carrier-based planes in the Royal Navy were second-rate. In the summer when Spitfires and Hurricanes were shooting the *Luftwaffe* out of the skies over Kent and Surrey, the navy flew old, slow, poorly-armed planes. The primary attack plane was the Fairey Swordfish, a fabric-covered biplane first introduced in 1936. The Swordfish was primarily a torpedo-launching aircraft, but could carry a small bomb load(3/4 ton). Its top speed was 140 miles per hour, but its slowness was an advantage for torpedo dropping. The Swordfish was powered by a single 690 hp radial engine. It carried a crew of three: pilot, observer/navigator, and gunner. On long missions, the gunner was dropped and his seat occupied by an auxiliary fuel tank. Pilots had flown the Swordfish for years, and were familiar with it; but the fighter plane coming into use in 1940 was a new model: the Fairey Fulmar. This at least was an all-metal monoplane, but the RN's requirement

Imperial War Museum Negative Number A 3538

Fairey Swordfish on Training Flight, 1943

that it carry a crew of two made this fighter plane a much poorer performer than its single-seat contemporaries. The Fulmar had a 1080 hp in-line engine, eight wing mounted machine guns, a top speed of 265 mph, and folding wings for carrier duty. The British had a long range reconnaissance plane available in the Mediterranean: the Short Sunderland, a 4-engine monster that had a range of 3000 miles. They also deployed a photo-recon unit on Malta flying the American-made Martin Baltimore. This twin-engine medium bomber could do 300 mph, which allowed it to fly over the base at Taranto taking pictures, and nothing in the Italian Air Force at that time could catch it.[5]

The Italian Air Force had a long history of excellence in aviation — winning prizes throughout the 1930's — but by 1940 many of its planes were getting long in the tooth. The primary attack plane was the Savoia-Marchetti S-M79: a tri-motor medium bomber that also could carry and launch a torpedo. The S-M79 had a maximum speed of 267 mph, and a range of 1200 miles. Unusually, it was built entirely of wood and featured a low wing; but the Italians made it work. For finding the Mediterranean Fleet, the Italians deployed two float planes made by the CANT company: the single engine Z501 and the tri-motor Z506. The former had a range of 1600 miles and a top speed of 171 mph; while the latter could make 226 mph over range of 1700 miles. The Italians produced some excellent single-seat fighters later in the war; but in 1940 they depended on the CR-42 built by Fiat. This biplane dated to 1938, was capable of 273 mph, but carried only two machine guns. More relevant to our story; the Italians did not develop night-flying capability by 1940.

Organization, Command, and Control

The key organizational issue was the centralized control of the Italian forces vs. the local control exerted by Admiral Cunningham over his fleet. The Italian naval high command, Supermarina, had its headquarters in Rome, together with the Army and Air Force commands. Orders went out from Rome to Taranto, other bases, and the Air Force planes flying recon over the Mediterranean; and information and reports and requests came back into Rome from these outposts. As a result, decision making was a slow process. Admiral Cunningham was an independent force, usually going to sea with the Fleet, calling his own shots. He had to work out cooperation with the Army and Air Force but, still, he was able to be far more decisive than was his Italian counterpart.

Cunningham commanded the ships of his fleet and the planes that flew from his carriers, but the photo reconnaissance unit established on Malta in September 1940 was an RAF operation. The RAF jealously guarded the pictures taken by these planes, and insisted that only RAF photo interpretation experts could handle them. Cunningham wanted up-to-date reports on the ships at anchor in Taranto harbor; but the finicky RAF rules on handling photos might have led to delays. Through a combination of courtesy and diligence, Cunningham would get what he needed.

War Breaks Out

The Italians declared war on June 10, 1940. At 6:57 a.m. the next day, bombs began falling on Malta. The Italians believed that bombing would render Malta useless as a British base, and so postponed the task of invading and conquering the island. The British and the Maltese suffered terribly under the bombardment, but held on stubbornly. Malta would remain an important British base, and later in the war aircraft and submarines operating from the island fortress would inflict heavy damage on Italian and German attempts to supply their armies in North Africa. In 1940, however, Malta could barely hang on. The Italians built up a large army in Lybia, and successfully ran troops, guns, ammunition, and other supplies through to that army from June to September: 150,000 tons of supplies and 13,000 additional troops made the trip without incurring any losses. The Italians despatched their large submarine force as the primary offensive weapon; but were disappointed with the results. Their subs tended to be very noisy, and thus, easily detected. They suffered heavy losses, and scored no hits on RN ships.

Cunningham wanted to fight, and brought out his fleet frequently to try to bring the Italian fleet to battle. In a brief encounter on July 9, 1940, the battle of Calabria (also called Punto Stilo), two large fleets exchanged gunfire for an hour or two. The Italian force consisted of two battleships, six heavy cruisers, 12 light cruisers, and many destroyers. Cunningham had *Warspite*, his flagship and his newest and fastest battleship, two other battleships, *Eagle*, six cruisers, and a destroyer screen. The battleships did most of the firing, with the Italians straddling some of the British ships; and the British obtaining one hit on the Italian battleship *Giulio Cesare*. Swordfish launched from *Eagle* were unable to score any hits from their torpedo attack; and Italian land-based planes bombed the British Fleet without apparent result, although it would later turn out that near-misses had damaged the aircraft carrier *Eagle*. The Italian admiral made smoke and turned away; and the British fleet did not have the speed to keep up.[6] This set a pattern for the rest of the year: when the British could find the Italians at sea; they would not stand and fight. A few salvoes would be exchanged, and then the Italians would flee. The Italians were getting their supplies through to Lybia; they neither wanted nor needed a stand-up fight. They followed the old strategy often used by a weaker force: the "fleet in being." The *potential* power of the Italian Fleet caused the British to waste time and fuel chasing them around trying to corner them, without risking the loss of the fleet in an actual fight. In the meantime, the Italian Navy could fulfill its support mission to the Army and Air Force units in North Africa. From June to October, Cunningham made 16 sweeps through the Mediterranean; "trailing his coat" before the enemy and inviting combat. He only sighted that enemy three times, and never brought on a significant fight.

Frustrated in his desire for a big-gun shootout, Cunningham turned to naval aviation to land some effective blows on the enemy. In July, Swordfish from *Eagle* attacked Italian vessels underway in the Gulf of Bomba.

Two Italian destroyers, *Nembo* and *Ostra*, were sunk, along with a freighter. Later in the month, *Eagle*'s airmen sank two more destroyers, *Zeffiro* and *Pancaldo*, the former at Tobruk, and the latter at Augusta. In August, the same aircrews accounted for the submarine *Iride* and the depot ship *Monte Garzano*. In September, *Eagle* was joined by the new carrier *Illustrious*. Together, they sank two freighters and a destroyer at Benghazi. In October, the two carriers struck again: this time hitting airfields and hangars on the islands of Leros and Rhodes.[7]

This summer of activity for the Fleet Air Arm demonstrated the power of naval aviation. The frequent stinging attacks by the planes of the FAA also took advantage of the passive Italian strategy. As long as the Italian Fleet stayed in harbor, the British carriers were free to roam the Mediterranean, striking at will against targets at sea and ashore. At the same time, the frequent action was improving the efficiency and skill of the pilots, seasoning them for attacks on larger and more important targets. It certainly began to dawn on Cunningham that naval aviation was the weapon most suited to his purpose; to bring the fight to his reluctant enemy, even into their home ports.

Cunningham Decides to Strike

By September of 1940, Admiral Cunningham found that several positive developments were putting him in a position to strike the enemy a heavy blow. The RAF unit from Malta was providing good intelligence on the harbor at Taranto and what ships were anchored there. His pilots were gaining experience and skill from action against smaller, less well-defended targets. The Italian reluctance to fight it out in a fleet battle left the initiative to the

British. To attack a fleet at anchor would simplify the navigational problem for the attacker, and deny the target ships the opportunity to maneuver while under attack. The old plans for an attack on Taranto - first drawn up in 1935 - had been dusted off and updated. Finally, his Fleet had been reinforced: another battleship, *HMS Valiant*, and two cruisers, *Coventry* and *Calcutta* joined the Mediterranean Fleet in early September. Along with them came a new carrier, *HMS Illustrious*, a powerful ship destined to become one the most famous fighting ships of the war.

Illustrious was the first of a new class of carriers specifically designed for combat in European waters where land-based aircraft would always be a threat. This meant that ruggedness was the prime feature designed and built into her. Her flight deck was armored - 3.5 inches of steel - unlike the wooden flight decks found on American and Japanese carriers of the time. She carried 16 dual purpose guns (twice as many as *USS Lexington*). These were 4.5 inch guns that could fire on enemy ships or planes. In addition, she had an anti-aircraft battery that included thirty-five gun emplacements. She was 735 feet long and 96 feet abeam at the waterline. She was equipped with radar, allowing her to spot incoming aircraft and launch fighter planes to challenge those attackers long before they reached the carrier's airspace. Ordered in January of 1937, launched in 1939, she went to sea in 1940 with all the tradition that the Royal Navy could muster: she was the fourth RN vessel to bear her name. In fact, one of her forebears, a 1803 frigate, participated in an 1809 attack on the Napoleonic Fleet at Basque Roads; an attack conducted at night against ships in harbor. The shakedown cruise in midsummer took *Illustrious* to Bermuda and back. Badly roughed up by severe weather on the outward portion of this cruise, *Illustrious* was repaired in Bermuda, replacing scuttles that had allowed a great deal of water to leak in

Australian War Memorial Negative Number 302415

HMS Illustrious with a Swordfish on the flight deck

during the rough Atlantic storms. Her aircrews used the better Bermuda weather to gain some flying time; they especially practiced evading fighter attack by stalling and maneuvering the slow Swordfish. During one such practice, the British fighter pilot playing the role of "enemy" crashed into the sea when the Swordfish he was following seemingly stopped in midair and stepped aside. *Illustrious* was back in her Scottish home port on July 26, 1940.[8] Fully fueled and stocked up, she received her planes and pilots, twelve Fulmar fighters and twenty-four Swordfish on August 11. On the 19th, Admiral Lumley St George Lyster, who had written the Taranto attack plan while aboard *Glorious* in 1935, reported aboard *Illustrious* to take up his duties as Rear Admiral, Aircraft, Mediterranean. On August 22, *Illustrious* floated down the river Clyde, bound for Alexandria.

After a brief lay over at Gibraltar, *Illustrious* joined the fighting war when she sailed as part of Force F on August 30. With her were the three other Alexandria-bound ships, *Valiant*, *Calcutta*, and *Coventry*. Joining them was Force H, the regular Gibraltar-based flotilla. Under the command of Admiral James Somerville, this fleet included *Ark Royal*, *Renown*, *Sheffield*, and 12 destroyers. This large force would escort a three-ship supply convoy to Malta; and *Illustrious* would fly six replacement Swordfish and a large shipment of spare parts to the tiny Malta air force. Force H came as far as Sardinia, where nine of *Ark Royal's* Swordfish attacked an Italian airfield. Somerville turned back for Gibraltar while Force F made a night run through the straits between Cape Bon and Sicily. Waiting for them south of Malta was Admiral Cunningham and the Mediterranean Fleet. They sent the supplies into Malta - including a second convoy that Cunningham had escorted from Alexandria - and the pilots of *Illustrious* made thirty flights to and from Malta to deliver the new planes and spare parts. The now stronger Med Fleet then headed east, splitting to go both north and south of Crete, and later attacking Italian air bases on Rhodes and Leros. By 6 September, the Fleet was back in Alexandria.[9]

Back at the "office," Cunningham invited his new Aviation Admiral, Lyster, and the Captain of *Illustrious*, Denis Boyd, to sit down with the Fleet staff and chat about the "best way to annoy the Italians."[10] An air attack on the Fleet at Taranto was quickly agreed to be the very height of annoyance. Cunningham set a momentous date for the attack - October 21, Trafalgar Day - and told his officers to get busy on the details. Unfortunately, this chance to one-up Nelson on the 136th anniversary of his greatest victory went a-glimmering when a fire on *Illustrious'* hangar deck destroyed two planes and damaged five more.

As the fire had been put out with seawater, a huge clean up and repair job was necessary to put the aircraft back in service. Planes and engines were taken to bits, washed, oiled, and put back together. The delay reset the target day to the next favorable moon: November 11-12.

Meanwhile, the Italians were busy with plans of their own. Mussolini had met with Hitler at the Brenner Pass high in the Alps on October 4. His feelings hurt by the patronizing attitude of *der Fuerher*, *Il Duce* decided that he would order a demonstration of Italy's military prowess and surprise the Germans with a great feat of arms: the invasion of Greece. Although 40,000 men, 700 vehicles and 33,000 tons of supplies had been escorted from Brindisi to Italian-occupied Albania during the last two weeks of September, Mussolini kept the intended invasion from Hitler during their October talks. The invasion kicked off on October 28, and the continuing need for supply of these forces may have contributed to the concentration of the Italian Fleet at Taranto.

The Fleet Goes to Sea

The attack on Taranto was the culmination of a week's worth of complex ship movements covering the entire Mediterranean and involving British ships of every description.[11] From Gibraltar and Alexandria, the Royal Navy went to sea with two aircraft carriers, five battleships, nine cruisers, 27 destroyers, and eleven merchant vessels in three convoys. The warships came together and separated, operating in as many as five different task forces at one time or another. The Italians conceded this freedom of movement to the British, hoping to use air reconnaissance to divine the location of British units in time to counter attack. It is fundamental to understanding the results of the action to realize that the multiple movements on the part of the British confused the Italians and concealed the true intentions of Admiral Cunningham. The two sides were like prizefighters; one determined to press an aggressive attack, the other hoping to counter punch. In the event, the British landed a stunning blow, but not until a period of sparring had served to confuse and confound the opponent.

The "bout" opened on November 4, 1940 when the convoy designated AN6 sailed from Port Said, bound for Athens. Three merchant ships loaded with gasoline made up the cargo-carrying portion of the convoy, and they were escorted by the light cruisers *Calcutta* and *Coventry*, and destroyers *Dainty*, *Vampire*, *Waterhen*, and *Voyager*. This group of ships would travel slowly, limited by the poor speed of the loaded tankers; and sail in formation, the warships surrounding and protecting the cargo haulers. Their course would bring them around the eastern end of the island of Crete, and then northwest to Athens. At all times, they would be within the flying radius of planes based on the Italian-controlled islands of Leros and Rhodes.

The next day, 11/05/40, another British convoy put to sea; this one originating from Alexandria. Code-named MW3, it was formed on five merchantmen bound for Malta and three freighters destined for Suda Bay on the northern coast of Crete. Escorting this group were the cruisers *Ajax* and *Sydney*. This convoy would rendevous with the convoy AN6 at a point some 200 nautical miles north of Alexandria on the 6th of November. Sailing together around Crete, most of the warships would pass north of the island and continue west toward Malta - the exception was *Voyager* - while the freighters made their scheduled calls at Suda Bay and Athens. *Ajax* and *Sydney* put in briefly at Suda Bay to unload supplies before rejoining the others.

THE ROYAL NAVY ON THE MOVE
November 4-9, 1940

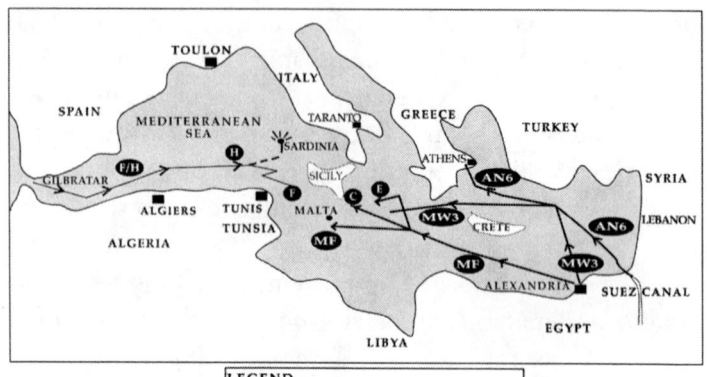

LEGEND
AN6, MW3, ME3 - CONVOYS
F/H - FORCES F & H SAILING TOGETHER
MF - MEDITERRANEAN FLEET
E - CONVOY ESCORT
C - CRUISERS

On 11/06/40 Admiral Cunningham took the Mediterranean Fleet out of Alexandria, minus *Eagle*. The old carrier had begun breaking down; probably due to damage caused by Italian near-misses in the battle of Calabria, and was finally judged unfit for this cruise.[12] Several of Eagle's pilots and planes were transferred to *Illustrious*. Cunningham's force was a powerful one: battleships *Warspite*, *Valiant*, *Malaya*, and *Ramillies*; cruisers *Gloucester*, *York*, and *Orion*; and destroyers *Nubian*, *Mohawk*, *Jervis*, *Janis*, *Juno*, *Hyperion*, *Hasty*, *Hero*, *Hereward*, *Havoc*, *Ilex*, *Decoy*, and *Defender*. At the center of the fleet would be *Illustrious*, with her radar probing the skies for Italian snoopers and her Fulmars up on combat air patrol. The fleet would steer northwest, and making 20 knots or better, catch and meet up on the 8th with the Malta-bound components of the earlier-departing convoys.

On 11/07/40 the Royal Navy got into action at the other end of the Mediterranean Sea. A number of ships departed Gibraltar, all of them warships. These were formed into two flotillas, the first designated Force H, which included the aircraft carrier *Ark Royal*, the cruiser *Sheffield*, and destroyers *Faulkner, Duncan, Firedrake, Forester, Fortune,* and *Fury*. The other was code-named Force F, and these ships would run through the straits and stay with Cunningham's Med Fleet. Force F included battleship *Barham*, heavy cruiser *Berwick*, light cruiser *Glasgow*, and destroyers *Encounter, Gallant, Greyhound,* and *Griffin*. All were under the command of Admiral Somerville. *Glasgow* and *Berwick* carried troops assigned to reinforce the garrison at Malta.

By the 7th of November then, the British were at sea in force. Battleships, carriers, cruisers, and destroyers were moving in at least three different directions in vastly separated sectors of the Mediterranean. Eleven merchant vessels were on their way to three different ports. By dawn on the 8th convoy AN6 was practically tied up at Pireus, the port of Athens; convoy MW3 was between Crete and the Greek mainland, emerging into the Ionian Sea on a westerly course; the Med Fleet under Cunningham was north of Benghazi, steaming northwesterly toward Malta, and Force H and Force F were north of Oran, heading east-northeast toward Sardinia. What's more, the Italian High Command was aware of most of this information.

By the evening of the 7th, *Supermarina* had learned from spies that British warships had left Gibraltar and Alexandria. The challenge for the Italians was to track the movements of these ships, deduce from that track the intended destination, and take steps to frustrate those intentions. Accordingly, at dawn on 11/8/40 orders went out from Rome for recon planes on Sardinia and Sicily in the west; and Leros and Rhodes in the east, to get up in the air and find the British fleets. This was accomplished with striking efficiency. At 1230 on the 8th the RDF screens on board *Illustrious* lit up with blips indicating incoming planes. The planes were detected at a range of 60 miles, giving the British fifteen to twenty minutes warning. *Illustrious* kept two or three Fulmars airborne at all times, and these could be directed on a course to intercept the Italians. More fighters scrambled off the flight deck within minutes. The Italians were flying CANT 501's and 506's: seaplanes with great range and speeds of about 200 mph. The British fighters were faster and better armed. They successfully chased the Italian planes away, and *Supermarina* received only sketchy reports; but they did locate a major British fleet 200 miles ESE of Malta.[13] An hour or so later, a similar situation played out in the skies above the British ships from Gibraltar. The Italians sighted the fleet about 100 miles north of Algiers, but again the British fighters rose to challenge and chase the Italian planes. The Royal Navy was taking to sea for the first time the system of air defense which Fighter Command had perfected in the Battle of Britain. RDF (called Radar by the Americans) detected enemy planes and allowed commanders to guide fighters directly to them. Thus, no fuel or time was wasted in a search for the attackers. The enemy, having already come some distance from his base, used up precious fuel trying to fight through the fighter interceptors. Only a fraction of the attacking force made it to the target, where it was still attacked by the fighter force. No other navy in the world operated such a system at the time, and it was a great advantage to the British throughout this operation.

Having located the enemy, *Supermarina* directed that he be attacked. At 1630 on the 8th, bombers appeared on the RDF screens of *Illustrious*. They were S-M 79's, identified at a range of about 30 miles. They were loaded with

Illustrious Contacts with Italian Aircraft

11/7/40	1130	Shadower on RDF at 25 miles, no radio report overheard
11/8/40	1230	Shadowers detected 17-20 miles out at 6,000 feet, 2 Fulmars launched, contact made, damage both sides
	1400	Shadower detected 25 miles out, fighters up, no contact made, fleet position reported
	1600	7 bombers incoming at 12,000 feet; fighters engage at 30 miles out, one bomber shot down, the rest jettison bombs and retire
	1700	3 bombers identified by RDF, fighters chase off
11/9/40	0930	3 planes on RDF at 22 miles out, they retire
	1100	Shadower reports fleet position
	1600	Shadower closes to within 12 miles, fighters engage and destroy
11/10/40	1300	Shadower discovered at 20 miles out, fighters up, engage and destroy
	1430	8 bombers discovered 65 miles out, fighters engage at 25 miles, damage one, remaining seven planes press attack, *Valiant* straddled

Source: Opie's 11/14/40 report

bombs, and planned a high level attack on the British ships. The Fulmars of 806 Squadron rose in time to challenge the Italians long before they could make a bombing run. One was shot down, while the rest jettisoned their bomb loads and ran for home. This pattern would persist throughout the operation: the Italians could locate the British naval forces, but their planes could not linger very long in the airspace controlled by *Illustrious* and her fighters. They could not press their attacks through the fighter umbrella, and a complete identification of number and types of ships was impossible given the short time available for observation.[14]

Still, as darkness deepened on the night of the 8th, *Supermarina* knew that two large British fleets were converging from the west and east; that both included aircraft carriers; and that a convoy was headed west to Malta. More warships were present than necessary for convoy escort; but what the mission of these ships might be remained obscure to the Italian High Command. Orders for the 9th called for more of the same: get planes in the air to find, identify, and attack the British.

Those British had their own plans for the 9th, and they got off the first punch. Planes from *Ark Royal* launched at dawn to attack the airfields of the *Regia Aeronautica* near Cagliari on the island of Sicily. The Swordfish of squadrons 810, 818, and 820 bombed the Italian base. The Italians retaliated later that same day, sending high-level bombers over Somerville's force, which by then was about 125 miles north of Bizerte. Staying at 20,000 feet offered the S-M 79's some protection from *Ark Royal's* fighters, but sacrificed accuracy of the bombing. Still, near misses caused some minor damage to *Barham*, *Ark Royal*, and *Duncan*, although the British were not slowed, and steamed ahead at 20 knots toward the Pantelleria Straits.

As for Cunningham, he was cruising on a northwesterly course, located approximately 100 miles south of Malta by the late afternoon of the 9th. Italian snooper planes had made contact in the morning and again around noon, but had been promptly chased away. The job of snooping was about to get even more difficult, for on the 9th Admiral Cunningham split his fleet into three task groups. The battleship *Ramillies*, along with three destroyers, broke off to escort the MW3 convoy into the Grand Harbor at Malta. Four cruisers - *Calcutta, Coventry, Gloucester*, and *York* - were ordered to sweep the seas north of Malta in order to contact any Italian ships that might venture out of harbor. The remainder of the Med Fleet - *Illustrious*, three battleships, and fourteen destroyers - continued on a northwest course toward the Sicilian Narrows to meet the oncoming Force F from Gibraltar. These multiple movements of British ships seemed to puzzle the Italians. The High Command received "various and conflicting reports"[15] of the location and movement of Cunningham's ships. Most of the ships were sighted, though not all were correctly identified.

While the Italians worried and wondered what these movements implied for the coming days, a small cloud appeared on the British horizon. On the afternoon of the 9th one of the Swordfish experienced engine trouble on takeoff and crashed into the sea. The 2-man crew was promptly rescued by one of the screen destroyers, but the plane was lost. This diminished the strike force by one plane (out of 24); but, more importantly, the loss of the aircraft meant that the engine failure would go unexplained, since no analysis of the wreckage would be possible. Later in the day, a second plane was lost in the same manner. Having lost *Eagle* before the mission even began, the British could ill-afford any further weakening of their striking power.

Over in the western Mediterranean, Admiral Somerville spent most of the day on 11/09/40 sailing due east toward Sicily. There had been no further attacks by Italian planes since the morning's near-misses by the high level bombers. The Italians certainly knew the location of these ships, but held back further attacks. Late in the day, the British flotilla reversed course and began to steam due west. At midnight, they reversed again, and began a high speed run through the narrows between Sicily and Tunisia. Their course was limited by the narrow channel, and would require them to travel close to the Italian-held island of Pantelleria. *Supermarina* was not fooled by the back-and-forth course changes; on the evening of the 9th five submarines and four destroyers were ordered into the Narrows to challenge the British ships. Unfortunately for the Italians, the subs were on the wrong track, and the destroyers, having no radar, sailed past the oncoming RN ships without detecting them. By morning, Force F, the reinforcements for Admiral Cunningham, had safely traversed the Narrows. Three destroyers from Force H who had acted as minesweepers for Force F turned around and returned to Somerville's fleet. Before departing for Gibraltar, Somerville ordered three Fulmars from *Ark Royal* transferred to the Malta air defense force.

By 1200 on the 10th, Force F - *Barham*, *Berwick*, *Glasgow*, and four destroyers - had joined the Med Fleet under Cunningham. The rendevous was completed at a position about 100 miles southwest of Malta. The four cruisers which Cunningham had despatched the day before to circle Malta had returned reporting no contact with enemy ships. *Berwick* and *Glasgow* carried 2150 soldiers for the garrison at Malta, and on the afternoon of the 10th they were ordered into Valetta to disembark these reinforcements. Cunningham remained south of Malta, cruising now with a very powerful force: five battleships, one

THE ROYAL NAVY STRIKES
November 10-11, 1940

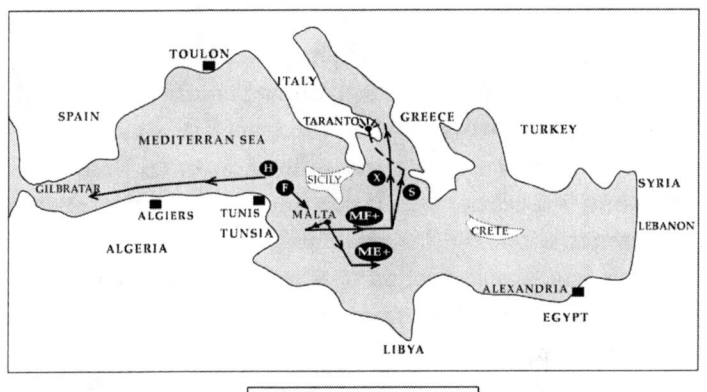

```
LEGEND
ME3   - CONVOY
F     - FORCE F
H     - FORCE H
X     - FORCE X
S     - STRIKE FORCE
MF+   - REINFORCED MED FLEET
```

carrier, eight cruisers, and 21 destroyers. The British took the Italian Fleet seriously, and had assembled quite an armada to strike at it.

Supermarina continued to be aware of the presence in the central Mediterranean of so many British warships. A report from the station on Pantelleria described eastbound British warships seen in the early morning of the 10th, but Rome received no further information.[16] A CANT 501 recon plane found the British Fleet on the 10th but was quickly shot down by *Illustrious'* fighter cover. An Italian submarine fired a single torpedo at *Ramillies* as she escorted convoy MW3 into Malta. The torpedo missed.[17] An attack on Cunningham's Fleet by 10 Italian bombers was broken up by the Fulmars flown off of *Illustrious* during the afternoon of the 10th; no damage was sustained by the British ships. Thus, through the 10th of November, the Italians were successfully tracking the movement of the British Fleet, and making infrequent and unsuccessful attacks on that Fleet.

Despite the poor showing of the Italian aircraft against his carrier's air defense, Admiral Cunningham had reason to be discouraged. On the afternoon of the 10th, another Swordfish experienced engine failure and crashed. Like the earlier two, this plane was from 819 Squadron. All planes from this group were ordered to drain their fuel tanks and inspect the fuel. It was found to be contaminated with water, sand, and fungus. Further investigation traced the problem to a single fuel tank on *Illustrious*. There was ample fuel in the other storage tanks to support the mission. British commanders could rest easy now that the cause of the engine failures had been found.[18] Unfortunately, the attack force had now shrunk to 21 planes.

Also on the afternoon of the 10th, the empty merchantmen that had made up convoy MW3 were constituted as ME3 and left Malta, east bound for Suda Bay. Escorting were *Ramillies*, *Ajax*, *Sydney*, and a small destroyer screen. The convoy made a brief run due south from Malta, then turned east. At the same time, the Med Fleet was moving east-northeast, across the wake of the convoy. Thus, Cunningham placed his fighting ships between the convoy and the Italians. Italian reconnaissance maintained contact with the Fleet during these movements, despite continuing aircraft losses.

By the morning of the 11th, the Mediterranean Fleet, augmented by the newly arrived ships of Force F, was in a position about 100 miles east of Malta, sailing on course almost due east. The convoy ME3 was about 100 miles south of that position, also east bound. Force H was retiring toward Gibraltar, at a point approximately 150 miles northwest of Bizerte, and heading west. At this time, the Italians appear to have relaxed, possibly concluding that the British operation was over and all ships returning to base. At the very least, their recon began to lose touch with the British. A report came in sighting east bound British ships, but including no ship types or numbers. A bombing squadron sent out later on the 11th could not find a target.

Admiral Cunningham was now moving fast. Orders went out to create two task forces from out of the ships in the Fleet. The first of these was built around *Illustrious*, and was designated "Strike Force." It included, in addition to the carrier, the cruisers *Gloucester, Berwick, Glasgow* and *York*; and a four-destroyer screen. Late in the afternoon of the 11th, Strike Force would separate from the Fleet, and run at high speed northwards toward a point from which to launch the attack aircraft. The second task group was designated "Force X"; it consisted of the cruisers *Orion, Sydney*, and *Ajax*; and the destroyers *Mohawk* and *Nubian*. This group would break away from the Fleet before Strike Force did; and run northward along the left flank of Strike Force. Thus the ships of Force X would be sighted first by any Italian recon planes that might be out. If undetected, Force X was to proceed further north and enter the Straits of Otranto leading into the Adriatic Sea. There, they might create a diversion by attacking Italian shipping moving to and from Albania. Force X was commanded by Admiral Pridham-Wippel.

The plan called for *Illustrious* to depart from the fleet at 1800 on the 11th; then cruise at high speed on a northerly course so as to reach the launching point - designated "Point X" - by 2000. This launch point was a position 40 miles west-southwest of Cephalonia; giving the pilots a 170-mile trip to Taranto.

While the Fleet on the afternoon of the 11th was preparing to execute these intricate maneuvers, the aerial reconnaissance unit from Malta was busy over the target. Squadron 431 flew over Taranto on the morning of the 11th, as it had every morning for several weeks. The pictures indicated that all six of Italy's battleships were berthed in the Mar Grande - the larger, outer harbor - at

Taranto. A large number of cruisers and destroyers were seen in the inner anchorage: the Mar Piccolo. The British kept another plane in the air south of the harbor all day long; to keep an eye out for ship movements in or out of the port. Previous photo missions had shown the installation of barrage balloons and torpedo nets, but these jobs were incomplete. Careful analysis by photo experts at Cairo led the British to conclude that the planes could fly through the balloon barrage; and that the incomplete torpedo nets would not protect the target ships. On the prior day, the 10th, a Swordfish piloted by Lt. Charles Lamb flew to Malta to bring back to the carrier the latest available photos. He was told to spend the night and leave in the morning with the fresh prints. He had a very successful stay: cleaned out a group of RAF pilots at the poker table, picked up a large bag of potatoes requested by Lyster, and flew off early in the morning with the needed pictures.[19]

As *Illustrious* and her 8-ship escort group steamed north toward Point X, the pilots who would execute the attack gathered for their pre-flight briefing. The attack was to be made in two waves, and pilots received their assignments and place in the order of takeoff. The obstructions, defenses, and ship locations were thoroughly discussed, using the photos taken less than 36 hours earlier. The first planes over the target would be flare-droppers, who would fly along the eastern shore of the anchorage and drop their magnesium flares. Torpedo-carrying planes would make their attacks on a west to east track so the flares would silhouette the target ships. Also included in the attack were several bomb-carrying aircraft, which were to seek out targets in the Mar Piccolo, or among the shore installations. The mood of the pilots was high-spirited: when the briefing officer announced that the next topic would be the return flight and the recovery of planes, an unidentified voice called out, "Don't let's bother about that!"[20] The recovery point was to be 20 miles *east* of the launch point: further away from the target. Pilots would find the fleet by means of a homing beacon broadcast from *Illustrious*. The beacon was a narrowly a focused radio signal that circled the compass once a minute. Each pilot's watch was synchronized with the rotation of the beacon so that the movement of the second hand became an analog of the movement of the beacon. Upon returning, the pilot would tune his radio to the frequency of the beacon, and look at his watch to get a bearing back to the ship. The carrier was lit in various ways to assist the actual landing. Each side of the stern was lit by a red and green shaded light; visible only from directly behind the vessel. The carrier blinked the letters "P" and "S" to port and stern, and flame floats were dropped astern at regular intervals. The two waves of the attack would launch about thirty minutes apart; the first made up of 12 planes, including six torpedo planes, four bombers, - each carrying six 250-pound bombs - and two carrying 16 flares and four 250-lb bombs. The second was composed of nine aircraft: five torpedo-carriers, two bombers, and two with flares and bombs. All the planes were Swordfish.

During the several hours of the run to launch point, mechanics and armorers checked and rechecked the equipment. The torpedoes were set to run at 33 feet, while the average depth of the water in the Mar Grande was 49 feet. The safety settings required the torpedo to run for 300 yards before it would detonate. The torpedoes were to be dropped within 1,000 yards of the target ship; while the aircraft flew level at an altitude of less than 75 feet and a speed of 125 knots (144 mph) or less. The British had invented a trigger mechanism which would explode the torpedo either by contact with a ship's hull, or magnetically, by reacting to the ship's magnetic field. They called it the "Duplex Pistol," and used it at Taranto. In relatively shallow water, the great problem was keeping the torpedo from diving into the mud before it leveled out and ran true, but the Royal Navy had planned for this difficulty. A roll of wire connected to the nose of the torpedo played out as the torpedo dropped away from the airplane. The tension caused by the wire pulled up the nose, and though the wire broke before the torpedo hit the water, the result was a "belly flop" rather than a "nose dive." British torpedoes equipped with this device could launch torpedoes in water as shallow as 24 feet.[21] British sailors wrote messages in the oil coating on the warheads: "To Musso From Winnie," and "Best Wishes from *Illustrious* and *Eagle*."[22]

As *Illustrious* churned through the Mediterranean toward the launch point, the Italians prepared their defenses. Despite the confusion in Rome over British ship movements and intentions, an attack was considered possible by local commanders, and preparations made. All anti-aircraft guns were manned through the night, including shipboard guns. There were 21 batteries of 4-inch guns, 13 on shore and eight mounted on rafts around the anchorage. Eighty-seven heavy and 109 light machine guns were placed around the perimeter of the harbor. The guns aboard ship added dozens more to this total. The Italians had no radar, but placed great faith in sound detection equipment which would "listen" for the noise of aircraft engines. Twenty-two searchlights were placed along the shoreline. Torpedo nets were in the process of being installed: 4500 yards out of a planned 14,000 yards were in place on the date of the attack. Ninety barrage balloons were in place, but a storm in early November had blown down two-thirds of these. There was no shore-based smoke-making apparatus at Taranto. The Italians were ready for an attack; in fact, they were so ready that at 1955 on the 11th, the AA guns at Taranto roared into action in response to the air raid warning alarm. It was a false alarm, perhaps triggered by the engine noise of a Sunderland flying boat that the British had patrolling outside the harbor, watching for last minute arrivals or departures. Five minutes later, as the firing died down in response to the all clear siren, *Illustrious* turned into the wind and began launching her planes.

The 12 planes that made up the first wave of the attack were commanded by Lt. Commander N. W. Williamson. The planes were rolled out on the flight deck with their wings folded back, causing one pilot to observe that they more closely resembled "four-poster bedsteads"[23] than combat aircraft. The routine for each pilot and plane was the same: engine comes to life with a roar; the few gauges are checked by the strapped-in pilot; the intercom connection between pilot and observer is tested; the plane is rolled forward and the wings spread by deckhands with a slam; a man with a green light waves the signal; the throttle is opened fully; and the plane rolls down the pitching and rolling flight deck and lifts off. There was a bright moon that night, occasionally shining through the moderate cloud cover. The planes attempted to link up and fly in formation, but the clouds and the wind made station-keeping difficult. The open-cockpit planes kept climbing in an attempt to find clear air: 4000, 5000, all the way to 8000 feet. At this altitude it was bitter cold; but the pilots flew on. They could not fly any recognizable formation, but stayed generally together by glimpsing one another ahead or to the side through the breaks in the clouds. The pilots had the distraction of their work to help them deal with the unpleasantness of the long, cold flight; but no such solace was available for the observer, who had also to contend with the auxiliary fuel tank. Here is how one man described it:

> *One's back and head rested on it and it was the explosion of one of these that had set off the hangar fire three weeks earlier. The tank was hardly a morale-booster to have with you when going in to face intensive anti-aircraft fire.*[24]

At 2045, the air raid sirens at Taranto sounded again, and once again, itchy-fingered gunners blazed away at imaginary targets. This was another false alarm, and the all clear soon rang out over the anchorage. It would be another two hours before the real attack arrived. The planes remarkably did keep together, forming into single-file order for the final run into the target area; except for one pilot who, having lost sight of his comrades, thought himself to be a laggard and sped forward at high speed. He arrived by himself, ten minutes early.

His name was H. I. A. Swayne, a Flight-Lieutenant flying a torpedo-carrying plane designated L4M ("L" for *Illustrious*). The noise of his engine triggered the sound detectors, and the air raid alarm sounded for the third time. Once again, the AA guns opened fire; and this third false alarm of the evening may have discouraged the Italian gunners, who had no way of knowing that the authentic attack was only minutes away. They did not hit Swayne, and the bright light of the tracer shells provided a beacon for the rest of the attackers, saving the problem of any last-minute navigation. It was now 2302 on 11/11/1940.[25]

The flares were dropped by Lt. L. J. Kiggell, flying plane L4P. They were set to ignite at 4500 feet, and float slowly down to earth via a parachute. Sixteen of them were dropped, from the four o'clock to the one o'clock position on the circular harbor above the eastern shore of the Mar Grande. The torpedo planes would fly in from west to east to make their attacks; and the flares would silhouette the target ships. Kiggell, having completed his mission, flew off to the right, searching for a likely target for his small load of bombs. Following him was Lt. Charles Lamb, the back-up flare dropper. Kiggell identified the oil tank farm on the southern edge of the base, and both planes dropped their bombs on the inviting oil storage tanks. Between them, they dropped 2000 pounds of bombs, igniting the oil into a large fire.

Lt Comm Williamson led the six torpedo-carrying planes across the open water of the harbor. The planes glided in at first, losing altitude quickly and hoping to elude the sound detectors. Most of them would hug the northern shore of the Mar Grande on their left, then turn slightly to the right to fly south-southeast at the battleships *Littorio*, *Vittorio Veneto*, and *Caio Duilio*. At a height of 1000 feet or so, they restarted the engines and flew down to the waterline, leveling out at 100 feet or less. They would have to maintain a low and slow flight, vulnerable to all those AA guns, for a minute or more before releasing their torpedoes.

Large parts of the anchorage were protected by barrage balloons, whose steel mooring cables could rip a plane to shreds if the pilot was unlucky or unwise enough to fly into them. However, the British pilots had been briefed on the barrage balloons, based upon the recon photos taken by 431 Squadron. The pilots knew where the balloons were as recently as 11/10/40; thirty-six hours prior to the attack. They also knew that the cables were 300 yards apart, and a Swordfish had a wingspan of 16 yards. They were prepared to fly around or through these obstructions.

Through or around the cables they went, breaking off from the single-file formation to approach from many bearings, in the hope of confusing and dividing the AA fire. Lt. Williamson flew over San Pietro Island and then due east. Through heavy AA fire, he headed for a group of battleships berthed at the southeastern corner of the anchorage. Two planes followed him in on similar courses: Lt. Sparke in plane L4C, and Sub-Lt. Macauley in L4R. Dipping to the right and then turning back to his left, Williamson leveled off on a northerly bearing and identified the older battleship *Conti de Cavour* directly ahead. Boring in low and level, he released his torpedo and achieved a hit. The torpedo struck on the ship's port side, beneath the forward main gun turrets. Williamson's joy was short-lived, however, for gunners on *Cavour* took their revenge by shooting him down before he even got out of the harbor. The plane went down with a splash. *Conti de Cavour*, a ship that had been completely rebuilt in 1937, was severely damaged.

Behind Williamson flew Sparke and Macauley. They flew straight on toward the battleship group, taking a generally easterly course. Anchored north of *Cavour* was *Andrea Doria*, another reconditioned battleship, and the outstanding new battleship *Vittorio Veneto*; both of them presenting their broadsides to the now leftward-turning planes. Sparke aimed for *Doria*, Macauley for *Veneto*; but both dropped at maximum range, and both missed. Completing a U-turn, the two pilots safely left the harbor on a westerly course.

Three more torpedo planes were in the first wave. The first of these was L4K, piloted by Lt. H. M. Kemp. Kemp crossed the breakwater at about ten o'clock on the circular harbor, flew toward the northern shore, then turned to his right to bear down on the northern group of battleships: *Littorio*, *Guilio Cesare*, and *Caio Duilio*. All these ships presented their broadsides to the north. Kemp identified *Littorio*, the other all-new battlewagon of the Italian Fleet; and bearing in close, put his torpedo into her side. Flying to the south from roughly the same starting point, Lt. H. I. A. Swayne - the early bird who had triggered the first air raid alarms - turned to his left and put a torpedo into the opposite side of *Littorio*. The final pilot, Lt. M. R. Maund, in E4F ("E" for *Eagle*), entered the harbor at the eleven o'clock position; flew along the northern shore, and then turned right and bore down on *Littorio*. He got his torpedo off, and it detonated in the mud of the harbor floor, only a few yards aft of *Littorio*. He didn't put a hole in the pride of the Italian Fleet, but he left a large dent. All three pilots escaped, despite flying through heavy AA fire.

Four bomb-carrying planes rounded out the first wave attack. Capt. "Ollie" Patch in E5A bombed the cruisers berthed in the Mar Picolo, the smaller inner harbor. He obtained no hits with his six 250-lb bombs. Behind him came L4L, flown by Sub-Lt. W. C. Sarra. He chose a much larger target: the seaplane hangar on the southern shore of the Mar Picolo. His bombs crashed through the roof of the hangar, and the subsequent explosions demolished it. Sub Lt. A. J. Forde in L4H tried to hit the smaller ships tied up side by side at the Mar Picolo jetty, but missed these destroyers. The final plane, E5Q piloted by Lt. J. B. Murray put a bomb into one of these destroyers, *Librecio*, but the bomb failed to explode.

By 2330, the first wave attack was over. Twelve planes had flown in, and eleven had flown safely away. Six torpedoes had been dropped, resulting in three hits and one near-miss. Extensive bomb damage had been done to the oil tank farm and the seaplane hangar. The only loss had been Williamson's plane. That officer, along with his observer/navigator Lt. N. J. Scarlett, struggled out of the downed plane and swam to a nearby floating dock. The Italians soon had them under arrest, though they were treated decently. All over the harbor, sailors tried to keep out the inrushing water; put out fires, tend to the wounded, and clean up the debris. Meanwhile, out in the skies over the Gulf of Taranto, the planes of the second wave attack were winging their way to the target.

These planes had taken off from *Illustrious* beginning at 2135, ninety minutes after the launch of the first wave. The plan called for nine planes to make the flight to Taranto and continue the attack, but the British ran into trouble when the eighth and ninth planes collided on the flight deck, causing enough damage to one of them that it was removed from the strike force. At 2145, then, only eight planes formed up in the air over *Illustrious* and flew off toward the target: five carrying torpedoes, two flare-droppers, and one bomber. By 2200, however, their number was reduced to seven when L5Q, a party to the flight deck collision, lost its auxiliary fuel tank and was forced to turn back. Flown by Lt. W. D. Morford, this plane was fired upon by AA gunners aboard *Illustrious* and *Berwick* as it approached the fleet. After being identified, the firing stopped, but an eyewitness reported that "the aircraft remained outside gunnery range for another 15 minutes, then made a cautious approach and was landed on."[26] The seven attackers flew on into the cold night, no doubt concerned over their own bad luck; and unaware of the success of their colleagues up ahead.

There was less than half an hour between the end of the first wave and the beginning of the second wave. Nervous Italian gunners kept firing at what they imagined to be targets throughout this interval. The seaplane hangar exploded and began to burn. The stricken battleships groaned and wallowed like wounded dinosaurs: *Littorio* punctured twice and rocked by a near miss, and *Cavour* taking on water from a huge hole in her port bow. Messages raced up and down the chain of command, both locally and between Taranto and Rome. The downed flyers, Williamson and Scarlett, had been captured, but English-speaking officers had to be found to begin the interrogation of the prisoners. To the Italians, then, there were not two distinct attacks, but only a barely noticeable lull in a single, nightmarish event.

The second-wave pilots had no trouble with navigation since the multicolored AA and tracer bullets lit up the sky over Taranto. This helped them to reach the target faster than their predecessors had; arriving over the harbor at approximately 2345. By this time they had been reinforced to eight planes. Lt. E. W. Clifford, flying the plane that had been scrubbed, had argued with his commanders to repair the plane and let him join the attack. He took off twenty minutes late, but flew directly to his target, the Mar Picolo, making up the delay en route.

At 2350 the flares were dropped to begin the second attack. As before, these were dropped above the eastern shore of the Mar Grande. Flying the flare-dropping planes were Lt. R. M. V. Hamilton and Lt. R. G. Skelton. Their primary mission complete, they turned to their right and dropped their bomb load - eight 250-lb bombs -on the oil tank farm that had previously been hit by Kiggell and Lamb. The AA fire was as heavy over land as it was over the water of the anchorage. Despite this, both escaped safely and started back on the long return flight.

Leading the torpedo-droppers of the second wave was Lt. Comm. J. W. Hale. Flying L5A, he swung to the north of the harbor, turning then to his right and crossing the waterline at the twelve o'clock position. This gave him a straight run at *Littorio*, and he pressed in close, dropped his torpedo, and scored the second hit on the starboard side of that unfortunate ship. Turning hard to his right, Hale exited on a westbound course flying out of the harbor over San Pietro Island. Next in line was L5H, flown by Lt. C. S. C. Lea. He entered the harbor at the eleven o'clock position, flew across the northern portion of the anchorage, then turned to his right to line up on the old battleship *Caio Duilio*, anchored astern of *Littorio*. He hit her, tearing a hole in her hull beneath the "B" turret on her starboard side. He also went into a hard, banking turn; and flying through the heavy AA fire, he left the harbor on a due west course. Close behind was Lt. F. M. A. Torrence-Spence, flying L5K. He flew the same course as Lea, but chose *Littorio* as his target. His torpedo missed, and he flew out on a southerly course, deciding not to attempt the tight turns of Hale and Lea. Lt J. W. G. Welham, piloting E5H, took the most roundabout course to his target. Flying completely around the northern edge of the harbor, he turned to his right and crossed the water's edge at the three o'clock position, flying west. He tried to execute a very tight turn and line up on *Vittorio Veneto*, but was unsuccessful. Continuing the tight turn, he looped around and flew west out of the harbor. The final torpedo plane, E4H, was flown by Lt. G. W. Bayley, with Lt. H. J. Slaughter along as observer. This plane was lost during the attack. Probably a victim of AA fire from the cruiser *Gorizia*, the plane exploded in midair. Bayley's body was recovered several years after the war; Slaughter's was never found.[27] The johnny-come-lately Lt Clifford, flying the patched-up L5F, arrived over the target just as the others were departing. He made straight for the Mar Picolo, and dropped his six 250-lb bombs on the ships anchored there. He achieved two hits: on destroyer *Passagno* and cruiser *Trento*. Like the earlier hits, these bombs failed to explode. Clifford then turned north to escape the target area, finally turning around to his right to return the way he had come.

The second wave attack was over by 0030 of the 12th. Seven of eight planes made it safely away from the anchorage. In the space of about ninety minutes, 20 aircraft had dealt a shattering blow to the Italian Fleet, and to Mussolini's imperial pretensions that were propped up by that Fleet. Three battleships had been holed below the waterline, one of these taking three torpedo hits. Eleven torpedoes had been dropped; five achieved hits on their target ships, with one very near miss. Black smoke from the burning hangar hung over the anchorage, along with the acrid smell of the exploded AA shells. The commander of *Caio Duilio* got his ship under way, and beached her to avoid sinking. Damage control parties aboard *Littorio* and *Conti de Cavour* struggled to keep the water out and patch the holes in the hulls of these two fine ships. All around the harbor, AA gunners rested at their guns, having shot off nearly 13,000 rounds at the attacking planes.[28] Bomb experts began to remove the unexploded bombs from *Passagno*, *Librecio*, and *Trento*. Work gangs began to clean up the dock areas. Though too busy for such a thought, the Italians might have reflected bitterly on the decision not to build an aircraft carrier; having witnessed first-hand the destructive power of naval aviation.

On board *Illustrious*, all was suspense and watchful waiting. No radio messages had been exchanged with the pilots, so on board ship no one knew of the their resounding success. The first wave had launched at 2000, and five hours later still had not returned. *Illustrious* was sending out its rotating homing beacon, and had dropped flame floats for the pilots to follow in a military version of Hansel and Gretel trailing bread crumbs. At 0112 the RDF screen lit up with planes: they were back! The planes circled once before landing, and the deck lights were turned on to assist them. First back on deck was Sparke, followed by Kiggell, Macauley, Maund, Kemp, Lamb, Sarra, Forde, Murray, Swayne, and Patch. All had landed safely by 0145, and the pilots gathered below to tell their tales to each other and anyone else that would listen. Air Operations Officer Beale carefully interviewed each pilot, skeptical of the optimism expressed by the returned flyers. The Senior Air Officer, Captain Robertson, also participated in the debriefing.

The second wave pilots returned around 0200. First to land was Hale, the flight commander. He went straight to his quarters, found the letter he had written for his wife in case he did not return, and destroyed it. He never revealed its contents to her. Following him in were Skelton, Welham, Torrens-Spence, Hamilton, Lea, and finally, of course, Clifford, who landed on at 0250. More debriefing ensued; followed by whiskey and eggs at 0300; sharing stories, arguing credit, happy to be alive, proud of what they had done.

At dawn on the 12th, *Illustrious* was heading south to rejoin Admiral Cunningham and the Med Fleet. This was accomplished by 0730. Rear Admiral Lyster planned a repeat attack for that night, and began to make assignments for such an attack. The pilots had been profoundly affected by the intense AA fire, and the attitude in the pilots' ready room was summed up by the comment, "They only asked the Light Brigade to do it once!"[29] The recon squadron was up over Taranto early in the morning, but commanders aboard *Illustrious* would not receive this information until midnight. Lyster did not propose to wait, so the Fleet remained in the area and planning for the repeat attack continued. Later on the 12th, the Italians found the Fleet and attacked, but without success. The Fulmars did their duty again, shooting down three Italian planes. Bad weather forced the cancellation of the repeat attack, and late in the day Cunningham ordered the Fleet to turn south and withdraw. Radio messages came in at 2031 and 2345 confirming the damage done to the Italian battleships. It concluded with "hearty congratulations on a great effort." Admiral Cunningham epitomized British understatement with his only message to *Illustrious*: "Maneuver well executed."

Also rejoining the Fleet on the 12th was Force X, under Admiral Pridham-Wippell. These cruisers and destroyers had happened along a convoy in the Adriatic, and sank four ships amounting to more than 16,000 tons.

The Fleet retired to Alexandria over the next two days, shadowed by Italian recon planes, and occasionally attacked by S-M 79 bombers. One of these put a bomb into destroyer *Decoy* on 11/13, but no other damage was sustained and the Fleet docked safely at Alexandria on the 14th.

THE OBSERVER

That same date, November 14, 1940, appeared in the upper right corner of page one of a memorandum sent to the Chief of Naval Operations (CNO) and the Office of Naval Intelligence (ONI), at the Navy Department, Washington, D.C. The rest of the heading was "American Legation, Cairo, Egypt." The document's subject was "British Attack on Taranto on the night of 11/12 November 1940". Its author was Lt. Commander John Newton Opie, III, USN. Enclosed with Opie's four-page report was a copy of the 12-page report which Captain Boyd had prepared for Admiral Lyster. Opie listed his duty assignment as "Assistant Attache, London." Who in the world was John Newton Opie, III? What was he doing in Egypt, writing up a report on his observations during his time aboard *HMS Illustrious* and enclosing secret Royal Navy documents?

Opie was a career naval officer; an Annapolis graduate in the class of 1924. He was born in Staunton, Virginia in 1903. His paternal grandfather had been a cavalryman in the Civil War, and wrote a book about his experiences.[1]

Opie grew up in Staunton and in Baltimore, where the family had a second home. He graduated high school in Baltimore, but secured his appointment to the Naval Academy from Virginia. He was tall and thin, and was a high jumper on the track team all four years. His classmates called him "Jack," and he boxed and played basketball, as well. Unusually for a midshipman, Opie was a teetotaler. His yearbook quotes him as proclaiming, "Drinking water never made any man a pauper nor any woman a widow."[2] He graduated ranked 114th out of his class of 522. His classmates included Edwin T. Layton, Hanson Baldwin, and F. L. Rhea. Layton would be Admiral Kimmel's Intelligence Officer in 1941 at Pearl Harbor; Baldwin would become the *New York Times* expert on naval matters, and Opie would marry Rhea's sister in 1926.

Upon graduation in 1924, Opie was assigned to duty aboard *USS West Virginia*. He cruised to Europe as a member of the battleship's officer complement, and in 1925 he and his ship joined the US Fleet on its cruise to Australia. He spent most of the next three years on duty in China. The US Navy maintained a flotilla at Shanghai, and sent gunboats up and down the Yangtze River in order to protect American citizens and American business interests. China in the 1920's was poorly governed, with regional warlords competing for control of territory, and only a very weak central government. Opie was aboard one of the gunboats, *USS Pigeon*, in 1926 and 1927. His ship took fire from hostile Chinese on many occasions as it patrolled the Yangtze, and often returned fire. In December of 1927, he transferred to the cruiser *Pittsburgh*, which was stationed at Shanghai. He served aboard *Pittsburgh* for about a year, then transferred to *USS Childs*, a destroyer. While aboard *Childs*, he returned to the USA. In June of 1931, he took up new duty at the Naval Torpedo Station in Alexandria, VA. He served there for three years, and in 1933 he began a series of short tours aboard auxiliary vessels: the hospital ship *Relief*, the oiler *Brazos*, and the repair ship *Medusa*. From 1935 to 1937 he served aboard the *USS California*, a battleship based at San Diego. In June of 1937 he took up another shore position: in the Design and Drafting Division at the Naval Gun Factory located in the Washington Naval Yard. In May 1939 he became Gunnery Officer aboard *USS Philadelphia*, an Atlantic Fleet cruiser. His cruiser was sent to the West Coast in the summer of 1939, and moved on to Pearl Harbor in April 1940. Opie was

Opie's Passport Photo

there in May of 1940 when he was suddenly called to Washington.[3] He traveled to Washington, DC in 7 days(fairly speedy for 1940), spent three days in the Office of the Chief of Naval Operations, and then found himself on the liner *SS Washington*, in civilian clothes, on his way to England to take up a secret job as Naval Observer.[4] He sailed from a Canadian port, and dressed in mufti because of the Navy's concerns about his mission violating the Neutrality Act. His passport bore a large pink notice headed "WARNING" which reminded him that travel in combat zones was illegal under the Neutrality Act. He would soon disregard that warning entirely.

Opie reported for duty in London on June 11, 1940 to the US Naval Attache, Captain Alan G. Kirk, USN. Kirk had been lobbying since the outbreak of the war in 1939 for a greater exchange of information between the Royal Navy and the US Navy. Senior officers in both navies - along with their political bosses - fought against this idea. While each side understood the *theoretical* value of information received from the other; each side put more emphasis on the value of *actual* secrets in their own possession. Top officials believed that they had more to lose than gain by trading secrets; they refused to authorize the exchange being proposed by younger officers like Kirk. This hesitancy to exchange information was broken down by the course of the war in Europe. When Hitler's panzers overran France in May of 1940, both American and British doubts about cooperation and information exchange vanished. Suddenly, the flood gates were opened, and all manner of technical information began to flow between the two navies.[5]

Opie was the first American officer to be assigned the duty of Naval Observer. Prior to Opie's arrival, Kirk had three officers working for him. By the end of 1940, there were 30 Naval Observers scattered around the Royal

Navy: in staff departments, at bases, and aboard ships at sea. These officers usually came over because of a technical specialty and confined their observations to the technical field in which they had experience. The records do not indicate why Opie was chosen, but it is possible that he was meant to look into mines and minesweeping.[6] The German magnetic mine was an innovative and highly secret weapon when it was introduced in late 1939. The British had revealed details of its design and construction to the US Navy in the middle of May; just the time Opie was plucked out of his cruiser. He was probably identified for the mission by Captain Jules James, the Assistant Director of Naval Intelligence. James had been the Commanding Officer of *USS Philadelphia*, and, thus, Opie's boss, until October of 1939. Although Opie had never served in minesweepers, his work at the Torpedo Station in Alexandria and the design/drafting shop in Washington, D.C. gave him some relevant experience. After arriving in London, this experience became irrelevant as he began to do what Kirk's staff had been doing: travel around England visiting military and industrial sites to learn how the British war effort was getting along. As an "extra" man, Opie had more time for these trips than did the regular members of Kirk's staff. Whatever the intentions were of the Navy Department, Kirk put Opie to work at this general task of observing and evaluating the war experience of the Royal Navy. Opie never wrote a report on mines and minesweeping, but in his first two months, he visited Portsmouth, Edinburgh, Glasgow, Bath, and Liverpool. He soon went beyond these "road trips" and went to sea. He was aboard *HMS Calcutta* from June 22 to 27, as the ship operated in the Bay of Biscay; and from July 17 to July 31 he was aboard several small warships on convoy duty along the eastern shore of England. These convoys were not "milk runs": the *Luftwaffe* was actively trying to sink ships and ruin harbors at this time. Opie wrote reports on his observations, which went to Kirk, his boss; and then went on to the Office of Naval Intelligence in Washington. Staff officers there would summarize Opie's reports - he was quite wordy - and send single-sheet notices around the Naval establishment. The usual addressees included the commanders of the main US Fleets (in 1940, there was organizationally one US Fleet; early in 1941, this was split into an Asiatic Fleet based at Manila, a Pacific Fleet based at Pearl Harbor, and an Atlantic Fleet based at Hampton Roads), the commanders of the staff bureaus such as ordinance, ships, navigation, etc; and the commanders of the 14 Naval Districts, or bases; and naval air commanders, both afloat on the carriers and ashore at the Naval Air Stations. Opie's first reports were not very flattering to the Royal Navy; he noted "sloppy ships and dirty sailors."[7] He admired the seamanship but questioned the fighting spirit that he saw among the officers and men; and picked out certain material and equipment items for praise: he liked the open bridge of a British destroyer, and felt that RN life belts and primer caps reflected superior design to those used in the USN. On his cruise in *Calcutta*, he witnessed a collision between that ship and HMS *Fraser*, a Canadian destroyer. Opie reported that the captain of *Fraser* was overtired and not mentally alert; he allowed his vessel to cross the bow of *Calcutta*. *Fraser* was cut in two and quickly sank. Opie's report included the recommendation that "...it must be worked out that the Captain can rest, even in time of war."[8] By embarking in the active-duty British warships, Opie had gone a step beyond what Kirk's staff had previously done to obtain useful intelligence about the Royal Navy at war. He took an even bigger step, a step clearly across the "neutrality" line, when he joined *HMS Illustrious* and sailed away from England on August 22, 1940.

His next report was dated August 29, which was a day before *Illustrious* reached Alexandria. Aboard ship, Opie had discovered RDF, the British version of what the American Navy called "radar." He quickly realized that the Royal Navy had something far better than the crude radar possessed by the Americans. His report states it is "essential install RDF in ships and recognition in all aeroplanes as soon as possible: otherwise bombs are first knowledge of attacking aircraft."[9] His use of the word "recognition" is a reference to automatic radio transmitters that the British had installed in their planes which identified the plane as friendly. The RDF operators could recognize planes, give distance and bearing, even count the number in a formation; but they could not tell friend from foe.

Once he reached the Med Fleet, Opie occasionally left *Illustrious* to embark in other types of British warships. He spent time in the battleship *Warspite*, destroyer *Jervis*, and cruisers *Sydney* and *Kent*. In fact, he was aboard *Kent* on September 17 when that ship was rocked by a torpedo dropped from an Italian S-M 79 aircraft. Opie reported that the plane came in at 200 feet or lower, that the torpedo was fitted with wooden fins that broke off when it struck the water, that it was magnetically triggered, and that it exploded "about 12 feet abaft the after part of the barbette of turret four and almost directly under the keel." *Kent* was severely damaged, and was towed back to Alexandria with great difficulty by the two destroyers that had been sailing in company with her. Opie later wrote a report on the damage control efforts by *Kent*'s crew; along with those of *Liverpool*, which was hit by an unexploded bomb around the same time. In November, he wrote a comprehensive report on entitled "Damage Control in the Royal Navy" that ran to 12 pages.[10]

Early on, Opie began a series of reports which he titled "Chronology of Events with the British Mediterranean Fleet." He produced these about every two weeks, and reported on all events, whether or not he was aboard the ship in question. He was frequently able to attach copies of official RN reports on these actions, usually from the officer in command. He also obtained and forwarded to Washington RN accounts of naval battles in the Mediterranean and elsewhere. At irregular intervals, he would pull together his personal observations, his interviews with British officers, and the available RN documentary material in order to deal at length with one subject. His reports generally took 45 days to reach Washington.

On the 5th of October, Opie sat down at his desk in the American Legation at Cairo and prepared for his typist a 20-page report covering a variety of topics.[11] The first of these was RDF. Opie's language leaves no doubt about how impressed he was with RDF and the fighter control system used aboard *HMS Illustrious*. The Royal Navy was taking to sea the same system of fighter control and direction that had won the Battle of Britain that summer and fall. Opie had never served in an aircraft carrier, so he may not have known how the set-up on the British carrier compared to that on American carriers (it was, in fact, far superior). Nonetheless, he could see immediately the value of the early warning of impending attack and the quick dispatch of fighter planes to meet that attack. Next, he reported briefly on the attack on *Kent*, and her escape to safety. He then dealt with horizontal high-level bombing, which he disparaged in strong terms. He had observed the Italians unsuccessfully making these bombing runs on units of the Med Fleet, but he was also probably influenced by the prevailing opinion among British pilots and air commanders that torpedo bombing was far more effective. He may also have picked up from the FAA men the idea that a determined attacker can expect to get through to the target. This was a widely-held prewar opinion: "the bomber will always get through." Opie repeated it here, in emphatic terms.

Over the next couple of weeks, Opie produced a number of further reports. He obtained British studies of two naval battles: the Fleet action off Calabria that took place on July 9, 1940; and the fight ten days later between *HMS Sydney*, accompanied by five British destroyers, and the Italian light cruisers *Bartolomeo Colleoni* and *Giovanni della Bande Nere*. He forwarded these British documents without adding any opinion of his own.[12] On October 19, he produced 15 pages on the tactical formations used by the Med Fleet. This report included many hand-drawn sketches with Opie's handwritten annotations.[13] On November 4 he wrote up a 12-page discussion of Damage Control in the Royal Navy.[14] He produced three chapters of his "Chronology of Events" series during this time, covering the time period 9/21 - 11/3/40.[15]

On October 14th, he had written up his observations on damage control aboard *Liverpool* and *Kent*. Curiously, he did not mention in this report that he was aboard *Kent* during the attack. There was still a bit of a cloak-and-dagger air to Opie's mission at this time. It appears that he wore civilian clothes when aboard the RN ships, because he notes in a later letter that most of his "clothing" was lost in the attack on *Kent*, and requests permission to buy replacement clothes. He never uses the word "uniform."[16] At about this time, Opie was seen by a State Department official aboard a British warship as she returned from a mission. The State Department man fired off an angry memo back to Washington complaining about this violation of the Neutrality Act.[17] Opie went right on doing what he had been doing, but probably tried to keep his profile low. On November 4, he wrote five pages on the British Mark XII 18-inch torpedo. In this report, he describes the methods used to prevent the torpedo diving deeply; especially the wire attached to the nose of the torpedo.[18] He mentions at this time that the Italians used wooden fins which broke off when the torpedo hit the water to accomplish the same result. Opie had been an eyewitness to these fins when he was aboard HMS *Kent*.

There were no nosy State Department men to pester him aboard *Illustrious*, so Opie embarked in the British carrier on November 6 as she set sail with Taranto as her target. Opie had the run of the ship, and he poked his nose everywhere. He looked over the shoulder of the RDF operator as pips appeared on his screen whenever Italian planes came within range. He stood in the 'goofers' gallery', a sort of porch built into the island below the bridge, and watched take-offs and landings. He lounged with the pilots in their ready rooms, patiently listening to the hair-raising stories all pilots love to tell of crashes and near-crashes. He prowled the hangar deck watching crews service, repair, refuel, and - after the contamination of the fuel supply - rebuild the aircraft. He saw the aerial photos taken of the Taranto harbor, and listened to the briefing of the pilots before they took off; and their debriefing after they had returned. So, he was well prepared to write his report when he returned to Alexandria.

He wrote four pages, and appended the 12 page report of Captain Denis Boyd.[19] Opie wrote under seven headings: Previous Training, Material, Instructions, Results, Enemy Opposition, Carrier Night Operations, and Lessons. Under the first, Opie mentioned the attacks earlier in 1940 on Leros, Rhodes, Tobruk, and Benghazi. He noted that all of these involved night flying, a very rare occurrence in the US Navy. He added that practice torpedo runs were made on Med Fleet ships while the Fleet was at sea. He also mentioned the "excellent air photos of ships, nets, defenses, and harbor of Taranto." He briefly described the torpedoes, bombs, and flares under his "Material" heading; also including a mention of the duplex pistol. It is doubtful that his stateside correspondent would have recognized that phrase. In his much longer section titled "Instructions" he laid out the plan of attack. He noted that the flare droppers and bombers were to distract the defenders, allowing the torpedo planes to sneak in and make their runs. He described the expected torpedo attacks: a determined flight through AA fire, dropping torpedoes at an altitude of 75 feet or lower while flying level at less than 125 knots and within 1000 yards of the target ship. He mentioned that the moon would be high and the position of the target ships such that moonlight would not be very helpful to the pilots. So, they would judge their altitude by the light of the flares. The pilots were also told to look for the barges that were mooring bases for the balloon barrage; and fly close to the barges to avoid striking the cables which held the balloons. Under "Results" he did not mention the post-action photos which confirmed the damages. These were not available aboard *Illustrious*, but would have been waiting in Alexandria when she returned. Opie must have heard that they confirmed the pilot's observations, but he was in such a hurry to write his report that he left the photo evidence out. What he did report was that the pilots were all sure that they had scored hits; the bombers failed to notice any explosions on the smaller ships hit; and the flares worked well but petered out in between the two waves of the attack. He did not mention the destruction of the seaplane hangar or the oil tank farm. Under his heading "Enemy Opposition" he noted that "hydrophones or other detection equipment gave warning" of the imminent attack because the enemy opened fire before the arrival of the attackers. He credited the many different attack bearings of the arriving aircraft for making the AA job more difficult. He stated flatly that the Italians did not use searchlights, but he noted that they did use colored tracers: red, green, white, and blue. He mentioned the damage sustained by several of the returning aircraft. He speculated that an RDF pip may have been one of the two planes that did not make it back; vainly trying to find the carrier. Under "Night Operations", Opie described the lighting used to support takeoff and landing. He mentioned the rows of small lights down the center and along each side of the flight deck to aid in taking off. He also described the neon batons used by landing control officers, and red and green lighted batons used to direct planes around the flight deck. He reported that each plane turned on its running lights and a light on the undercarriage near the tail hook just before landing. He mentioned the flame floats, blinker lights, and port and starboard lights used by the carrier. He did not mention the homing beacon.

Finally, Opie listed "Lessons" of the attack as he saw them. Number one was that "AA fire is not effective." Opie would repeat this observation throughout his tour of duty and would emphasize it again when he returned to the USA. It was probably his strongest impression from his combat experience. In 1940, it was an accurate impression. The density of AA guns on ships and around bases was low; the marksmanship of AA gunners was poor, and the quality of the guns was not very high. However, the crucible of war would force drastic improvements in AA performance in the next year or two, and Opie's strong opinion would be rendered obsolete by the course of events. In another report, Opie declared that "the only answer to attacking planes is defending planes." The course of the war would bear out the truth of this position.

Lesson #2 was that flying so low that ships would hesitate to fire on the attacking planes for fear of hitting comrades on the nearby ships was a useful tactic, especially for night attacks. His next lesson was a cautionary one:

Opie admired the determination and bravery of the British pilots, but he doubted that their performance could be matched. Mentioning that he saw the pilots personally before and after the attack, he stated that had the repeat attack originally planned for the night of the 12th been made, "It is doubtful in my mind . . . the pilots could have stood up under the strain and gone through the AA fire again." So although the AA fire was not effective, it had a powerful psychological impact upon the pilots who endured it.

Opie's fourth "lesson" was the broadest, and might have had the greatest impact had it been followed up. Here's how he phrased it:

> *The difficulties of defending ships on moonlit nights in a harbor are numerous and some believe it better to keep the fleet at sea on such occasions.*

Sailors had always considered their ships to be safest when in harbor, but the range and power of aircraft were challenging that age-old truth. The attack on Taranto was the first demonstration that ships might be safer at sea than in harbor. The enemy would know where to find the harbor: it's a fixed point. Ships cannot maneuver to avoid the attack. The ability of carrier-based planes to appear suddenly after traveling hundreds of miles meant that constant vigilance was required by the base defenders. This was a new method of war-making in 1940, and Opie recognized it, though, imperfectly, through a glass, darkly.

The final lesson Opie passed along to his bosses at the Navy Department was the British Navy belief about the relative value of different types of air attack on enemy ships. Opie reported that the Royal Navy had "definitely given up" high level bombing; and that they far preferred torpedo bombing to dive bombing. He noted that they feared the "loss of or correction of aim" during the long, steep dive. This comment was probably wasted on the US Navy, which had pioneered dive bombing and believed in it very strongly.

Opie continued at his paperwork while the fleet rested and regrouped at Alexandria. On the 14th he forwarded a British report on the Battle of the River Plate, where three smaller British ships had outfought the German pocket battleship *Admiral Graf Spee* in December 1939. Opie added his own evaluation: "the side which holds out the longest generally wins."[20] The next day he worked up a long report titled, "Construction Details of *HMS Illustrious*." He included sketches from the files of the ship; and exhaustive engineering details on all engineering equipment. He described the homing beacon used to assist pilots on their return flights, and he discussed the tradeoff between the protection provided by *Illustrious*' armored flight deck and the reduced striking power of her consequently smaller complement of aircraft.[21] Opie's next report was dated 11/20/40; a 12 page discourse on Anti-Aircraft Fire. Opie mounted his hobby horse again and railed at the ineffectiveness of AA fire. He asserted bluntly that, "Fighter aircraft is the weapon that is effective against enemy aircraft."[22]

Cunningham took the Med Fleet to sea on the 25th of November and again on the 16th of December, and Opie again sailed in *Illustrious*. Once again, the British Admiral 'trailed his cloak' across the Mediterranean, but only light skirmishing with the Italian Fleet ensued. At the end of December Opie wrote up a long report on British Tactics, including the use of RDF, torpedo attacks, lookouts, conduct of the Fleet during air attack by day and night, and direction of Fleet fighters in defense of the Fleet at sea.[23] In early January, Opie went to sea again, this time aboard the battleship *Warspite*. He must have counted himself lucky, for on the 10th, *Illustrious* was subjected to a savage attack by German dive bombers operating from bases on Sicily. The carrier was hit by several bombs, and thoroughly wrecked, but her steel flight deck protected her interior spaces, and she limped into Malta for repairs. Attacked again over the next several days, she was patched up enough to allow her to leave for Alexandria on the night of the 23rd, arriving safely on the 26th. She was later sent to the USA for extensive repairs and rebuilding.

Opie knew his time in the Mediterranean was coming to an end, and on January 16th he wrote a letter to Kirk, the attache at London. In this letter, he summarized his work to date, and suggested how he would like to continue the job in the months ahead. It is in this letter that Opie mentions his wardrobe problem, caused by the loss of his clothes when *Kent* was torpedoed. He tells Kirk, "I've literally been living in one suit. If I go by plane when I leave here I should be overweight if I started in buying things. However, if I stay the winter, it will be necessary to go ahead and buy some clothes." Opie makes these statements to explain why he had been pressing Kirk in previous letters as to the date of this return to England. He worried that Kirk would resent this pestering if it went unexplained. Opie then went on to show his boss that he had been hard at work. He listed 15 specific subject reports that had been completed and sent, originals and five copies enclosed. He mentions two reports that he was then working up: "...a summary of comparisons of British and American gunnery and a description of the training methods of personnel used in the British Navy." Then he returns to the subject of what he will do next. He first butters up the boss, thanking him for this assignment, "for I realize only too well that this is a swell job and I am content to stay here indefinitely...." Finally, he crawls out on a limb and puts forth his idea for his own future. He says, "...I feel that writing is a very inadequate way of getting war experiences home. I am not trying to drum up my own trade but I honestly feel that I should fly to Hawaii and talk to the boys there on war experiences and how to train to meet the lessons learned,...." After a stop in Washington, "to talk over design and material questions," Opie sees himself returning to England to dig more secrets out of the Admiralty. "Knowing the ropes there, I feel I could do it very easily." Then, "if it would not be asking too much," a return to the Mediterranean Fleet for more combat experience. Opie may have been asking too much, for his future held none of these hoped-for events.[24]

Opie stayed with the Med Fleet for about another six weeks. Since his official duty station had always been "Assistant Naval Attache, London," there are no orders in the record for his transportation, and thus, no record of exactly how and when he returned to London. He wrote a few more reports, extending his "Chronology" up to February 5. His last report to be sent from Cairo was a write up of the German attack on *Illustrious*.[25] This report is dated 3/6/41, and it includes Opie's own observations made from *Warspite*, and the available British records. On March 10, Opie is in London. On that date, he forwards a copy of the battle report of *Illustrious*' Commanding Officer.[26] He receives orders on April 2, 1940 to return to Washington, and he is detached from the Naval Attache's staff on that date. He departs England aboard *HMS Resolution* on April 5. After a stop-over in Iceland, he arrives at Philadelphia. He reports to the Chief of Naval Operations on April 23.[27]

On April 29, Opie made a presentation to the Navy's General Board. The General Board was a sort of advisory committee made up of recently retired admirals and the current heads of important Navy departments. In a brief lecture, Opie summarized for the Board his experience and conclusions after observing the Royal Navy at war for eight months. He tells them that he draws three "outstanding" lessons. These are:

1) Material differences between RN and USN are small
2) Fighting spirit is most important
3) Training must go on during war as well as before

He described RDF as the "greatest development in materiel." He described the armored flight deck of *Illustrious* and how it probably saved the ship from destruction. He reminded the assembled brass that the cost of the armored protection was a smaller complement of aircraft, and therefore, a reduction in striking power. His only judgement on this trade off was that time would tell. He enthusiastically repeated his many previous critical remarks about anti-aircraft fire. "AA gunnery is the bug-a-boo of this war," he pronounced emphatically. He asserted that determined pilots would always evade or survive AA fire. "The only answer against planes is planes," he concluded. The written report of his lecture was distributed throughout the navy, including copies going to Admirals Kimmel and King, the commanders of the Pacific and Atlantic Fleets, respectively.[28]

This lecture marked the end of Opie's career in Intelligence. He never got to make his trip to Hawaii to talk about his war experience with "the boys there." One of "the boys there" was the Pacific Fleet Intelligence Officer, Captain Edwin T. Layton. Layton was the officer charged with the responsibility of knowing where the Japanese Navy was at all times. He was a also a Naval Academy classmate of Opie's. It is easy to imagine that Layton may developed a different approach to his job after a few hours of chatting with Opie about what the Royal Navy accomplished at

Taranto. That conversation never took place. Instead, Opie was given a desk job in the Navy Department at Washington: Office of the CNO, Gunnery Section - Assistant AA Desk. After all his harping about the poor performance of AA fire in the Mediterranean War, Opie was now part of the solution to that problem. The "additional duties" listed on his Fitness Report were "Fire Control and Radar in connection with new construction." His boss in this job was Captain Willis A. Lee, Jr., who would later help Opie rebuild his career after it had foundered. Lee wrote glowingly of Opie in the Fitness Report dated 9/16/1941: "An officer of highest personal and professional character; has great initiative and energy....I consider him an outstanding officer in all respects."[29] This high praise helped Opie get the thing he wanted most: a command afloat.

On September 28, 1941 Opie assumed command of *USS Roe*, a *Sims* class destroyer. She was a new ship, launched in 1939. Displacing 1620 tons, *Roe* carried four 5-inch guns and eight torpedo tubes. As Commanding Officer, Opie was responsible for a complement of 192 men. In the fall of 1941 the ship operated in the North Atlantic, in and out of the ports of Boston, Halifax, Argentia Bay, and Hvalfjordur, Iceland. During this time an undeclared war with German submarines was being waged in these waters. The US Navy was on what FDR had christened "Neutrality Patrol," covering the waters between Iceland and the USA, and escorting convoys of merchant ships bringing Lend-Lease supplies to Britain. However, when a US ship spotted a German sub, it broadcast the sub's position and course. This was hardly a "neutral" act, since British and Canadian ships were monitoring these broadcasts. U-boat commanders were ordered to avoid conflict with US ships, but shooting did break out on at least two occasions. On 4 September *USS Greer* was attacked by torpedoes fired from U-652. *Greer* fought back, dropping depth charges, but neither side did any damage to the other. On 31 October, though, *USS Reuben James*, a destroyer escort, was sunk by U-552. Though the public outcry was great, Roosevelt refused to ask Congress for a declaration of war. Opie, in command of *Roe*, participated in this undeclared war. *Roe* helped escort three different convoys during October and November, but did not fire at or depth charge any German subs. On December 7, 1941 Opie awoke aboard ship in the Icelandic harbor of Hvalfjordur. The ship got under way by 0800, and tied up at a dock at the port of Reykjavik by 1000. Five hours later, the bombs began to fall at Pearl Harbor. Opie was no longer a neutral; the US Navy was now at war.

Opie stayed aboard *Roe*, and the ship stayed in the Atlantic, for about a year. In October 1942 he was transferred to an under-construction destroyer, *USS Bache*. Opie would supervise the completion of this new, larger ship, and then take her to sea as her first captain. As he assumed his new command, Opie was promoted to Commander. He arrived at the Bethlehem Steel yard on Staten Island on October 20, and took *Bache* to sea upon her commissioning on November 10, 1942. Opie's tour of duty as CO of *Bache* ended abruptly in January, 1943. He was relieved of command, apparently because of several problems aboard ship. Two that are found in the record include a lost torpedo, for which Opie was admonished, and a burnt-out boiler, which was the fault of a negligent sailor and his equally negligent lieutenant.[30] On January 20, 1943 Opie found himself back at a desk job at the Navy Department, but his career was rescued by an old boss, Rear Admiral Willis Lee, who immediately sent him on a six week inspection tour of Naval bases in the Pacific. Upon his return, he spent a month at a troubleshooting job in the Navy Department; and then landed a "real" job with the Sixth Amphibious Fleet, commanded by Rear

Admiral Alan G. Kirk, his old boss from London. Opie would enjoy success in the amphibious operations of the Atlantic Fleet for the rest of his WWII career. Promoted to Captain in June 1943, he went on to become Chief of Staff of the 8th Amphibious Force, and played a major role in the ANVIL landings in southern France in August of 1944. For this service, he was awarded the Legion of Merit and the Bronze Star. Injuring his back in early 1945, he came home to another Washington desk job in April 1945.[31]

Post-war assignments included Commanding Officer *USS Oakland*, a cruiser based in California, Chief of Staff of the 7th Fleet during combat operations during the Korean War, and a final stint with the Reserve Fleet at San Diego. He retired in 1954 at the rank of Rear Admiral. He lived in San Diego until his death in 1975.[32]

AFTERMATH

The raid on Taranto is now seen, with the benefit of hindsight, as a milestone in the development of naval air power. Aircraft extended the range of naval weaponry by hundreds of miles; and the Fleet Air Arm demonstrated at Taranto the power and significance of this fact. The extended range of naval striking power meant that bases previously considered out of the enemy's reach were no longer safe. Sailors had always felt that they and their ships were safe when anchored in a friendly port, but the wrecked Italian battleships at Taranto provided striking evidence to the contrary. Not all the world's navies were at war in November of 1940, but they all should have been paying attention. This study now turns to a review of how the other navies around the globe reacted to the news of British success at Taranto.

Italy

The most immediate and powerful impact of the Taranto raid was felt, of course, by the Italian Navy. As the sun rose on the 12th of November, the damage done by the Fleet Air Arm was made visible:

Littorio had three holes in her underside, was down by the bow and listing to starboard. On that starboard side, forward of her "B" turret, were two of the three holes: one 49 feet by 32 feet, and the other, further forward, measuring 40' X 30'. On her port quarter, the hole measured 23' X 5'. Her hull was dented on the starboard quarter from the explosion of Maund's near miss.

Caio Duilio had taken one torpedo, but had been able to get under way. Her captain beached her to prevent her from sinking. With her bow ashore, her stern was underwater from the after turret on back. The hole in her hull measured 36' X 23'.

Conti de Cavour had sunk. The torpedo that Lt Commander Williamson had launched, the first "shot" of the attack, had struck on the port bow, opening up a hole forty feet by twenty-seven feet. Two of her fuel tanks had flooded, and her main deck was awash.

Trento was leaking oil from the damage inflicted by an unexploded bomb, while both *Librecio* and *Passagno* showed fractures in their hulls from the same cause.

In addition, the seaplane hangar was a smouldering wreck, the tank farm had been severely damaged, and there was oil floating everywhere on the surface of the harbor. Shell casings littered the ground and the decks of all surviving ships; the Italians had fired off more than 12,500 rounds of Anti-Aircraft ammunition.[1]

The greatest casualty of the attack may have been the pride of the *Regia Marina*, but the Italians shrugged off the embarrassment and dismay and went to work. The Fleet was relocated to Naples, a harbor that was further away but considerably safer. For the remainder of the war, torpedo nets were deployed around all Italian ships in harbor, and smoke-making apparatus was added to harbor defense establishments. The Italians also made personnel changes, the most important of which was the recall from enforced retirement of Admiral Umberto Pugliese, the former Chief of the Naval Engineering Corps. This officer had been forced out of the navy by Mussolini because he was Jewish. After Taranto, *Il Duce* decided that Pugliese's experience and skill was vital to the salvage and repair of the damaged ships.[2] Pugliese did his work very well: *Littorio* was back in service by March of 1941, and *Caio Duilio* was fully repaired by May. *Conte de Cavour* was refloated in July, 1941 and then towed to Trieste, but she never was fully repaired.

It is often said that the greatest result of the attack was the damage done to Italian morale. Such statements usually will be found to come from British sources. Despite these claims that the Italian will to fight had been smashed as certainly as her battleships had been wrecked at Taranto, the Italian Navy performed well up until the surrender of Italy in September, 1943. They gained revenge for Taranto in December of 1941, when a squad of frogmen laid explosives beneath the British battleships *Queen Elizabeth* and *Valiant* while those ships lay anchored at Alexandria. Both ships were severely damaged and out of action for many months.[3] The Italians took major losses in the Battle of Cape Matapan in March of 1941. In a night battle, three heavy cruisers and two destroyers were sunk by British battleships equipped with radar. Italian losses ran to more than 3,000 men, including the Admiral in command. The British did rescue nearly 900 Italian survivors, and radioed the location of the disaster to Rome so that more could be picked up.[4] Still, the Italian Navy fought on, running supplies to North Africa frequently and successfully. Italian supply convoys lost only 9.5 % of material and 4% of men during the three years of the war. Guarding these supply convoys was the primary assignment of the Italian Navy. In the summer of 1943, the navy evacuated 70,000 men and 10,000 vehicles from Sicily despite overwhelming Allied superiority afloat and in the air. At the surrender in September, the Navy sailed most of its operational vessels to Allied ports, often fighting through stiff attacks from German aircraft and U-boats. The Italian Navy maintained its morale throughout the war in the Mediterranean. Fighting without radar and with very poor air reconnaissance, and having many of its operational plans identified by British radio interception(ULTRA), the Navy fought commendably in what can now be seen to have been a hopeless mismatch of a fight.[5]

Germany

Germany, allied to Italy in the Pact of Steel, seemed to be well placed to learn the lessons of Taranto. In truth, however, the alliance between the Germans and Italians was mostly a propaganda story: the two high commands never engaged in joint planning and operations. In contrast to the Americans and British, who began combined staff talks in January of 1941, nearly a year before the USA was even at war, the Germans and Italians planned their own strategy and seldom even notified one another in advance of the kick-off date of major operations. The attack on Taranto came near the end of a six-month period when German-Italian joint operations in the Mediterranean might have been upgraded to a realistic level. A number of senior German officers - especially the Navy Commander Admiral Raeder - advocated a turn South in the second half of 1940: to close the Mediterranean to British forces by seizing Gibraltar, Malta, and the Suez Canal. The opportunity existed there for Germany to seal off the entire southern frontier of her European empire, and to deal a shattering blow to the prestige and the commerce of the British Empire. Specific operational plans for the storming and taking of these three targets were worked up by the German General Staff. During August of 1940 a border dispute between Hungary and Romania, along with the movement of increased numbers of Russian troops to the Russo-Romanian border, threatened the security of the Ploesti oil fields, Germany's most important source of petroleum. Accordingly, plans were drawn for the movement of German army units into the client state of Romania. Planners began to link these army units with the earlier operations against Gibraltar, Malta, and Suez into a comprehensive plan for the neutralization of all threats from the South, including unfriendly states such as Yugoslavia, Greece, and Turkey as well as the British forces scattered throughout the Middle East. As this grand plan was developing, it was set back, and ultimately, set aside, by a series of disappointing developments, most of which were political in nature. Germany's allies - Spain, Italy, and Vichy France - all proved to be hesitant to cooperate with the ambitious plans of the German Staff. In October, Hitler himself traveled to meet with his supposed supporters: Mussolini at the Brenner Pass, Franco at Hendaye, and Petain at Montoire. Each of these meetings produced only waffling and trimming from the junior partners in the Axis. The Italian disaster at Taranto may have been the last straw, adding military disappointment to these earlier political let downs. Thus, the significance of

Taranto for the German war effort may well have been as a confirmation of Hitler's choice to turn away from combined operations in the Mediterranean with reluctant and ineffective allies, and pursue the goal he had set out for Germany years before in *Mein Kampf*: to attack and conquer the Soviet Union.[6]

On a tactical level, the Germans were quick to recognize the destructive power of air-launched torpedoes against ships. The Germans had no such capability; neither their small naval aviation force nor the mighty *Luftwaffe* had developed the planes, pilots, and procedures to add this sort of attack to their array of weapons. Hitler ordered the development of such a weapon almost immediately after news of the Taranto attack had reached Germany. The effort bogged down, though, in bureaucracy and inter-service rivalry. Goering jealously guarded his control of all aviation matters, despite the fact that the Navy should have logically been given priority in such a development. In the end, they never did produce an effective air-torpedo arm.[7]

In the short term, though, the Germans realized the need to send help to the Italians. Fleigerkorps X, a veteran unit relying mainly on Stuka dive bombers, was transferred to Sicily. Commanded by Albert Kesselring, this unit would become infamous to the Royal Navy.

England

The attack on Taranto was a tremendous boost to English morale, both in the Mediterranean and at home. Churchill was able to rise in the House of Commons and deliver good news, for a change. He said, "I feel sure the House will regard these results as highly satisfactory and as reflecting the greatest credit upon the Admiralty and upon

Admiral Cunningham,..., and above all on the pilots of the Fleet Air Arm..."[8] He also mentioned Taranto in his correspondence with FDR.[9] Cunningham's reward was short-lived; after the congratulatory messages came orders from London reducing the size of his fleet: *Ramillies* and *Malaya* were to leave the Med Fleet.

The greatest beneficiary of the Taranto success was the venerable Swordfish aircraft. It would continue in service throughout the war. In the attack role pioneered by the planes which flew on 11 November, the "stringbag" would play a major role in the sinking of the *Bismarck* six months later. Shifted to escort carriers, the Swordfish would become a terror to U-boats in 1942 and 43, playing a decisive role in the winning of the Battle of the Atlantic. Late in the war, the "obsolete" biplane would even be fitted with air-to-ground missiles.

The results for the pilots who flew off *Illustrious* that fateful night were less happy. They were first of all dismayed by the meager awarding of medals and commendations. Only two DSO's and 4 DSC's were awarded to the 42 men who had flown into Taranto's harbor that night. Fifteen of the 42 would not survive the war; killed in action during the remainder of the fighting.[10] For those that survived, the war gave them the chance to advance to better planes and bigger carriers; some even serving in the Pacific in 1945 alongside the great carrier task forces of the US Navy.

USA and Japan

The thirteen months between the raid on Taranto and the Japanese attack on Pearl Harbor were filled with decisions and actions that led to the tragedy of December 7, 1941. This study will examine Japanese and American reactions to the Taranto raid together and chronologically, in an effort to chart the evolution of planning and thinking about the security of fleets at anchor in what were traditionally thought to be "safe" harbors.

Yamamoto Isoruko, Commander of the Japanese Combined Fleet, and the man most responsible for the Pearl Harbor attack, had begun to think about aerial torpedo attacks against unsuspecting ships several months before the planes from *Illustrious* wrecked the Italian Fleet at Taranto. After training exercises in late April and early May of 1940, the leadership of the Japanese navy was impressed by the performance of their torpedo-dropping aircraft. Discussing the maneuvers with his Chief of Staff, Yamamoto wondered aloud about the chances of an attack on Pearl Harbor featuring torpedo aircraft.[11] Later, Yamamoto would move far beyond this "thinking out loud" moment.

At this same time, a large portion of the US Fleet arrived at Pearl Harbor. Normally based at San Diego, the American navy was on its own annual maneuvers at sea in the waters around Oahu from April 10 to May 9. Expecting to go back to the West Coast, the navy was surprised when the President decided to keep the Fleet at Hawaii. FDR and his advisors felt that a strong naval force stationed at Pearl Harbor would help to deter Japanese aggression into South East Asia. In the end, the Japanese were not deterred. In fact, Yamamoto felt compelled to attack the US Navy because he decided that it threatened the flank of Japan's great movement into Southeast Asia. The raw materials that Japan needed were there for the taking, including oil, tin, rubber and rice. For Yamamoto, the American Fleet at Pearl Harbor could not be ignored: it must be smashed.[12]

American naval leaders first learned of the Taranto attack while reading the morning newspaper. The *New York Times* put the Taranto raid into a six-column headline in the November 14, 1940 edition. The *Washington Post* treated the story with the same emphasis. *TIME* spread a long story and a large map over 3 pages in its November 25th edition. The number one man in the US Navy, Chief of Naval Operations Admiral Harold R. Stark was particularly impressed by the news of the Taranto raid. He immediately began hounding his subordinates for more information, for analysis of the British success and its implications for American ships at anchor, and he wrote directly to his commander at Pearl Harbor, Admiral James O. Richardson. On November 22, only ten days after the Taranto raid, Stark sent a letter to Richardson which cited Taranto and worried about the defense of the fleet at Pearl Harbor. He inquired of Richardson whether it might be practicable to place anti-torpedo nets around the ships berthed there. Richardson answered in the negative, citing the restricted space in the anchorage and the distance of the mooring spots from the entrance. This last comment indicates that Richardson was thinking of submarine-launched torpedoes when he answered Stark. Stark did not pursue the matter.[13]

At the end of November, a new officer transferred in to the War Plans Division of the Office of the Chief of Naval Operations at Washington, DC. Walter C. Ansel, recently promoted to the rank of Commander, had been working in the ROTC program at Harvard University, but he wanted duty that was "more Navy", and jumped at the chance to add a staff job in the nation's capital to his service record.[14] It is an old service adage that "stuff" rolls downhill, and so Ansel, as the most junior officer, got the assignment to study Pearl Harbor's defenses as a result of Stark's worrying over the matter after Taranto. Ansel began working on the project even though his own superior officers - especially War Plans Director Richmond Kelly Turner - did not share Stark's anxiety. Ansel's first problem was to get reliable information out of his opposite number at Army Headquarters concerning the specific composition of Army personnel, equipment, guns, and ammunition in Hawaii. After many weeks of effort, Ansel's work resulted in a letter from the Secretary of the Navy, Frank Knox, to the Secretary of the Army, Henry Stimson. The letter, dated January 24, 1941, details the woeful state of Hawaiian defense forces and offers suggestions concerning necessary reinforcements and improvements. It concluded:

> *Your concurrence in these proposals and the rapid implementation of the measures to be taken by the Army, which are of the highest importance to the security of the Fleet, will be met with the closest cooperation on the part of the Navy Department.*[15]

Meanwhile, back in Japan, Admiral Yamamoto had in December hardened his thinking about attacking the US Navy at Pearl Harbor. Convinced that such an attack must open any potential war with the USA, Yamamoto began in January to bring the idea to other officers in the Japanese Navy. On January 7, 1941, he wrote to the Navy minister, Oikawa Koshiro, outlining in brief his thoughts and asking to command the forces that would make such an attack. Five days later, he shared the same thoughts with Onishi Takajiro, Chief of Staff of the 11th Air Fleet, Japan's premier naval aviation outfit. Yamamoto asked Onishi to begin studying the idea, keeping it secret as much as possible. The attack on Pearl Harbor, then, began as a belief by Yamamoto that it was strategically necessary. After a month or so of thought, Onishi - having consulted only 2 other officers - returned to Yamamoto with his verdict: very difficult, but not impossible. The Japanese would later study Taranto very thoroughly; but the example of the Royal Navy was irrelevant to the basic decision made by Yamamoto: "to decide the fate of the war on its very first day."[16]

On January 9, 1941, Opie's report on the Taranto raid arrived via diplomatic pouch at the Office of the Chief of Naval Operations. It was summarized down to one page by Lt. Commander Herbert F. Eckberg. After a brief listing of facts - such as number of planes launched and returned, level of pilot training, torpedo depth and speed settings, and level and effectiveness of AA fire - Eckberg repeated Opie's five "lessons learned": a) AA fire is not effective, b) attackers should fly low between ships to discourage shipboard AA from firing, c) mental strain on pilots in such attacks is very great, d) ships might be safer at sea than in a harbor, and e) the Royal Navy was abandoning high-level bombing against ships, preferring torpedo attack or dive bombing. This one-page summary was distributed widely in the US Navy. The Commander of the US Fleet (then Admiral Richardson, soon to be Admiral Kimmel), and the Commander of the Atlantic Fleet (Admiral King) were primary addressees. Also on the distribution list were the Bureau of Ordinace, the Aeronautical Bureau, The Marine Corps, the War College, the War Plans Division, and the Office of Naval Intelligence. Eckberg's summary was dated February 14, 1941.

Back in Hawaii, big news was about to break. On January 5, Admiral Richardson learned that he was to be relieved of his command. Richardson had fought hard against the basing of the Fleet in Hawaii. For logistical reasons, he wanted his ships and sailors back in San Diego. He was right on the logistics: the Navy was very short of oilers; the entire fuel supply for the Fleet had to stored (above ground) on Oahu; regular replenishment from California tied up ships and men; and shore facilities at Pearl Harbor were far inferior to what the Navy had built up over many years in Southern California. Richardson was loud and blunt about his belief that it was a mistake to keep the Fleet in Hawaiian waters. The President was determined to do just that. After two meetings between the men, in July and October, FDR decided that he needed an Admiral who would at some point shut up and obey orders. On February 1, 1941, Richardson was officially relieved by Admiral Husband E Kimmel. At the same time, the position of Commander, US Fleet was abandoned, in recognition of the fact that one man could not effectively command three forces scattered all over the globe. Accordingly, Kimmel was to be Commander, Pacific Fleet (CinCPac); while Admiral Thomas Hart became Commander, Asiatic Fleet (CinCAsia), based at Manila; and Admiral Ernest J King became Commander, Atlantic Fleet (CinCLant), based at Norfolk.

One of Richardson's last acts was to endorse and send to Washington a lengthy memo on the defense of the base at Pearl Harbor and the ships of the Fleet anchored there. The report was written by Admiral Claude C Bloch, Commandant of the 14th Naval District. The Naval District represented the permanent facilities and those personnel attached to them. The Fleet came and went, but Bloch's command was responsible for the base and the defense of that base. In his memo, Bloch listed area after area where he was under-equipped to do the job. He had too few planes and ships to conduct an effective anti-submarine patrol; he would have to depend on the Army's RADAR net to warn of incoming attack planes, *if* it ever became operational; he had no fighter planes or AA guns, and the ones the Army had were few and feeble; and he had barely enough men to protect the base facilities from sabotage. Bloch's bleak description of his command's ability to defend his base and the Fleet might have stirred Washington into action had not Richardson soothed the alarming report with his endorsement. Richardson threw buckets of cold water on the idea that any attack from any enemy was a realistic possibility; mentioning "the improbability of such an attack" several times. What's more, he said, until the Army could beef up its forces, the Fleet could defend itself; using shipboard guns and carrier-based planes to respond to the highly unlikely event of an attack. Thus, the report that went off to Washington on January 7, 1941 was little noticed by its readers, who paid more attention to the calm and reassuring endorsement than to the worrying and scary list of shortcomings that came after it.[17]

So, on February 1st when the US Navy implemented its reorganization, the worry over the safety of Pearl Harbor that Admiral Stark had felt when he first heard of the Taranto attack had dissipated and a chance to apply the lessons of Taranto had been missed. A few days later, on the 7th, Secretary of War Henry Stimson responded to the January 24 letter from Navy Secretary Frank Knox. Though Stimson was forced to acknowledge the accuracy of the feeble state of Hawaii's defenses portrayed in Knox's letter, he asserted that Hawaii was the strongest, best-equipped of all the Army's foreign bases. He promised continuing improvements through the next 6 months, including the construction of a network of radar stations for Oahu. On the same date, General Marshall wrote to the Army commander on Hawaii - Lt. General Walter C. Short - emphasizing that the Number 1 mission of the Hawaiian Department was the protection of the Fleet. Unfortunately, over the next ten months Short would forget this command, and become increasingly worried over the threat of sabotage and the security of Army bases and weapons from local attack. Even though his reports to Washington clearly showed his obsession with sabotage and local defense, he was never again reminded of the primary mission of protecting the Fleet and its Naval Base at Pearl Harbor.

The final fruit of Stark's concern for the safety of Pearl Harbor after he learned of the Taranto attack was a memorandum sent by the CNO to CinCPac, Admiral Kimmel, on February 14, 1941.[18] The subject was "Anti torpedo baffles for protection against torpedo plane attacks, Pearl Harbor." Stark spends three pages in this memo re-hashing the discussions he had previously had with Admiral Richardson about the practicality/necessity of placing protective nets around the ships of the Fleet at Pearl Harbor. His opening paragraph mentions the shallow water and the congestion of the harbor as factors weighing against the need for such protective nets. He states that "a minimum depth of water of seventy-five feet may be assumed necessary to successfully drop torpedoes from planes." (The depth of water in Pearl Harbor averages 40-50 feet). He then reviews the problems getting the ships of the Fleet quickly and conveniently in and out of their anchorages and allowing "tugs, fuel oil barges, and harbor craft" to maneuver alongside individual ships. He notes that the terrain surrounding the harbor and the availability of shore based AA fire, balloon barrages, and fighter aircraft may also lessen the need for protective nets. He states that the attack at Taranto was made in water 84-90 feet deep. He finally mentions that available nets are expensive, heavy, and take up a lot of space. After this long and mostly negative review of the subject of nets to protect ships in harbor from torpedo attack, Stark closes thus: "Recommendations and comments of the Commander-in-Chief are especially desired." Kimmel took the hint: he never pursued any kind of torpedo net, and he remained convinced - until December 7th - that aerial torpedoes would not run in the shallow waters of Pearl Harbor.

On the same day that Stark's letter to Kimmel went out, the intelligence summary of Opie's Taranto report was distributed. Although Stark had been worrying out loud about the implications of the Taranto attack for two months, no one in the Navy Department ever seems to have mentioned to him that Opie was aboard *Illustrious*; or that his report on the attack had arrived in Washington in early January. Opie's report was silent on the depth of water at Taranto, and the Navy leadership seemed to consider this the only important factor; so perhaps this explains the poor use of what Opie did say. Had he been asked, Opie would probably have been negative on torpedo nets, but he would have been loud and forceful on radar and fighter aircraft. He might also have mentioned that the best way to safeguard the fleet would be to keep it at sea; and he would have been shocked to learn that most ships would be at anchor every weekend.

Although Washington seemed uninterested in Opie's report, the "real" Navy out in the field was paying very close attention to the war in the Mediterranean. On February 18th, Admiral John McCain (the grandfather of the US Senator of the same name) writes a "Dear Spike" letter to Admiral Blandy, the Chief of the Bureau of Ordinance in Washington.[19] McCain opens his letter with a mention of "recent reports" regarding "belligerent naval activity in the Mediterranean." The subject of the letter is the problems preventing the arming of US Navy patrol aircraft (such as the PBY) with aerial torpedoes, and the relevant "belligerent naval activity" would seem to be the success of the Italians and their S/M 79 planes. This was the plane that had torpedoed *HMS Kent* when Opie was aboard her (see page 52). This letter shows that the working Navy was aware of events in the European War, and was thinking through the implications of those events for the US Navy. The "thinking" Navy of staff officers in Washington was dismissive: on February 24th, an officer named T. D. Ruddock answers McCain, advising him to not "give too much credence to reports coming from abroad because the technique of all belligerents appears to be greatly to over emphasize the importance of their own weapons."[20]

More relevant to our story was the reaction to Opie's Taranto report by one USN officer: Admiral Aubrey W. Fitch. Fitch was the Commanding Officer of Carrier Division 1; and one of the Navy's most experienced naval aviators. He had earned his wings in 1930, and in the ensuing decade had served almost exclusively in aviation commands. On March 3, 1941, Fitch made 55 copies of Opie's report, including the attached report of Captain Boyd, RN; and sent them off to practically every senior officer in the Navy.[21] On June 21, another senior Admiral expresses himself on aerial torpedoes: Admiral William F. Halsey. Writing from Pearl Harbor, Halsey - Commander Aircraft, Battle Force, US Pacific Fleet - asks the Chief of the Bureau of Ordnance to speed up work on torpedoes for the aircraft of his carriers.[22] Citing "the evidence from Europe", Halsey asserts that "torpedoes may prove more effective than bombs as the primary striking weapon for carrier aircraft." These three examples show that line officers in the US Navy were aware that the British and the Italians were sinking ships and doing great damage with air-launched torpedoes. These officers worried that our Navy was far behind in this important area; and wanted to see improvements made quickly. In contrast, the staff officers in Washington focused on depth of water and decided that the threat from air-launched torpedoes was not very great. When they did consider defensive measures, these staff officers thought of static defenses like nets, baffles, barrage balloons, or smoke making equipment. Opie's reports looked to active defenses such as radar, fighter aircraft, and maneuvering the fleet out of danger before an attack could be made. In early 1941, the US Navy still had 9 months to prepare for the coming Japanese attack, but the clock was ticking.

Meanwhile, the Japanese were methodically working on Yamamoto's attack plan; diligently trying to improve the accuracy of their bombing, the effectiveness of the torpedo planes, their techniques for re-fueling at sea, the tactics of their fighter squadrons, and dozens of other specifics of the attack plan. Given an over-reaching goal by their commander - destroy the US Fleet suddenly and completely on the first day of the war - the small number of capable and experienced officers aware of the plan bent to their tasks with maximum effort. No navy in the world trained as hard and as realistically as did the Japanese. Because of this, no navy suffered more casualties during training. As the days ticked off toward December 7th, the Japanese Navy was applying itself with the thoroughness and attention to detail that would later establish the reputation of Japanese manufacturers. The two officers who had the most to do with the training and preparation of the Fleet would survive the war and disagree about the relevance of Taranto to their task. Commander Genda Minoru was the chief air staff officer of the First Carrier Division. Composed of *Akagi* and *Kaga*, this was "the first team" among Japan's aircraft carriers. Genda played a very large role in planning the Pearl Harbor attack and conducting the training that led up to it. After the war, Genda stated that Taranto "had no influence on the Japanese preparations," attributing the Japanese success to grueling hard work and trial-and-error training that eventually solved the very tough tactical problems like refueling at sea and dropping torpedoes in shallow water.[23] Commander Fuchida Mitsuo was a combat pilot who commanded the first wave attack. When discussing the British attack at Taranto, Fuchida told a post-war interviewer that, "I learned very much from this lesson in shallow water launching."[24] In fact, both officers were correct. Genda was right that only a tremendous effort by Japanese technicians and pilots solved the shallow-water problem; an effort that Genda oversaw and led. Fuchida was right that the lessons of the Taranto attack were studied by the Japanese. The link between Taranto and Pearl Harbor is the contact between the Japanese and Italian navies that took place over the intervening year. Genda may have been unaware of the nature and content of this contact, or may have chosen to ignore it in order to emphasize the strenuous and diligent effort of the Japanese.

These contacts began in November 1940 when a staff officer serving as an attache in Berlin, one Naito Takeshi, flew from Berlin to Taranto to inspect the damage and discuss the attack with Italian Navy officers. Although any report that Naito may have written and sent back to Tokyo was destroyed like so many other Japanese records, we have Fuchida's statement that he discussed the Taranto attack with Naito in October, 1941 when Naito's duties brought him to the base where Fuchida was assigned. This conversation, which carried on over a day and a half, was likely where Fuchida "learned very much" about the Taranto attack.

Fuchida's chat with Naito came too late to have much significance for the development of plans and tactics for the December 7th attack, but an earlier contact between Japanese and Italian Naval officers began in May. On the 18th of May, a full Naval Mission, headed by 2 admirals and involving more than two dozen officers, arrived from Japan in Rome.[25] Over the next few days, the Japanese officers met 4 times with their Italian counterparts, in sessions lasting more than 10 hours each. After wrapping up their business in Rome, the mission traveled to Taranto, where the Japanese admirals were photographed aboard *Littorio*, still under repair. Discussions at Taranto concentrated on torpedo doctrine and tactics. The mission returned to Japan in June. Since the solution to shallow-water torpedo dropping eventually adopted by the Japanese was fitting a wooden fin to the torpedo that broke off on contact with the water and reduced the depth that the torpedo dived, and this was the very same method used by the Italians (see page 52-55, where Opie reports this about the torpedo which struck *HMS Kent*), it seems highly likely that the idea came back from Italy with the Japanese Naval Mission. The Japanese had previously experimented with such wooden fins, but the Italian experience would have confirmed the value of this approach. Genda's men still had to struggle and work to make the idea effective, but must have been encouraged by the report of those meetings in Italy.

By the time that the Japanese and Italians were conferring at Taranto, Jack Opie was back in Washington, DC. Settling into his new job, Opie busied himself with plans and designs for AA gun emplacements on new ships. As the war went on, ships were designed to carry more and better AA guns, the firing of which was linked to better radar sets. The navy would develop and deploy the proximity fuse, an AA shell that actually contained a radar set of its own, allowing it to "know" when a target was close and explode at the right moment. By 1943 or 44, Opie's lament that AA fire was ineffective would no longer be true, and his emphasis on AA fire may have diverted his career from torpedo matters and the safety of ships in harbors; where his observer experience would have been better utilized.

Down the hall at the Navy Department, others were considering these matters and the result was a remarkable memo that went out to the Fleet over Admiral Stark's signature on June 13, 1941.[26] What was remarkable about the memo was that it took back advice given to base commanders only a few months earlier. In February, Stark had told Kimmel that "a minimum depth of water of 75 feet" was necessary for air-dropped torpedoes to run successfully. Since Pearl harbor allowed only a depth of 45-50 feet, Kimmel presumed - until December 7th - that such torpedoes could not be used in any potential attack on his ships. The June memo (from Stark, but signed by the Assistant CNO, Adm. Royal Ingersoll) explicitly retracts the earlier advice:

> *Recent developments have shown that United States and British torpedoes may be dropped from planes at heights of as much as three hundred feet, and in some cases make initial dives of considerably less than 75 feet, and make excellent runs. Hence, it may be stated that it cannot be assumed that any capital ship or other valuable vessel is safe when at anchor from this type of attack if surrounded by water at a sufficient distance to permit an attack to be developed and a sufficient run to arm the torpedo.*

The purpose of this memo was, presumably, to reverse the earlier message that shallow water harbors were safe from aerial torpedo attack. The memo, unfortunately, weakens that primary message by throwing in several distracting ideas, such as the mention above of space - undefined space - around the ship to allow an airplane to run in and allow the torpedo to run off its safety distance and arm before striking the target. The memo goes on to say that "while no minimum depth of water" can be considered to provide safety, depth of water will be a consideration for the attackers, and attacks are "more likely" in deep water(60 feet) than in shallow water. As did the earlier memo, this one reports that the Taranto attack was made in water of 66-72 feet deep. Unlike the earlier memo, this was not addressed to Admiral Kimmel, but to the Commandant of the Naval District, Admiral Bloch. Admiral Kimmel, however, received a copy.

What did get Kimmel's attention in April and May was the reduction in the size of his Fleet by orders transferring some of "his" ships to the Atlantic Fleet. In April, he lost *Yorktown*, one of his three aircraft carriers, and 5 destroyers. In May, more transfers cost him three battleships, four cruisers, and seventeen destroyers, along with oilers, transports, and other auxiliary ships. FDR and Admiral Stark were very worried about the success of German U-boat attacks on the convoy traffic to England, and so ordered these transfers. Kimmel came to Washington in June, and at a meeting with the President argued forcefully - and successfully - for no more transfers. During his week-long stay in Washington, Kimmel was in and out of the Navy Department building many times. So was Jack Opie, but they never met.

The Japanese continued to drill and to train for the Pearl Harbor attack. In settings resembling the Hawaiian harbor, pilots flew practice runs over and over again; not knowing the target that they were simulating. Engineers and testers worked out a wooden fin that successfully reduced the initial dive of the torpedoes by September 1, but manufacturing the new weapon would take another few months. In the end, the modified torpedoes were delivered to the carriers in November, only days before the Japanese Fleet sailed on the cruise that would take them to infamy.

In late July, the Americans would handle another report from the Mediterranean that had implications for the safety of the Fleet at Pearl Harbor. As had happened in February, the officers out on active duty were sensitive to new weapons and tactics arising from the European war; and the staff officers in Washington missed the point. This story begins in San Diego, where the War Plans staff of the 11th Naval District began to study the safety factor of shallow water; asking the pilots in the torpedo squadrons based at the Naval Air Station how deep torpedoes would dive before running true. The pilots' answer was 10-12 fathoms, or 60-72 feet. Somehow this question was referred to Lt. A. K. Morehouse, assigned as an observer to HMS *Ark Royal*, operating from Gibraltar. Morehouse answered it on 7/15/41 in a memorandum received in Washington on 7/22/41. Morehouse reported as follows:

> *Records of the RN 18-inch Mark XII indicate that this torpedo may be dropped in water as shallow as 4 fathoms. This shallow dive is only possible when the torpedo is set in low speed (27 knots) setting. In high speed setting torpedo dives to approximately 3 fathoms beyond its depth setting. In low speed setting, six feet deeper than the set depth is the average launching dive.*[27]

This report arrived in Washington one week after Stark had sent his wishy-washy memo to the Fleet retracting the 75-foot standard from February. Stark's June memo (see page 85) had said rather timidly that "in some cases" torpedoes dropped from as high as 300 feet would make dives of "considerably less than 75 feet." Now, the Office of Naval Intelligence had word from one of its men with the Royal Navy that British torpedoes could be successfully dropped in *24 feet* of water! Nothing ever came of it: no further warning went out to the

Fleet; and Kimmel would testify to the Congressional Committee investigating the Pearl Harbor attack that he never believed that aerial torpedoes could be successfully dropped in the 50 feet or so of water in the Hawaii anchorage. The reason why Morehouse's report disappeared may be typographical. Page one of the report listed the contents of the reports in four numbered items. The comment about depth of water was item # *five* on page three: it had been left out of the "contents" list. Busy staff officers may have just missed it. In fact, it may never have been read until the author found it in 1991 at the National Archives.

And so December 7th came, and the good work of Opie and other observer officers went to waste. Opie never made his proposed trip to Hawaii to talks things over with "the boys there." It is tempting to consider what might have been had he done so. The man who had looked over the shoulders of British sailors as the RDF screens lit up with blips showing Italian recon planes, and listened as radio operators directed the fighter planes on to those targets, would have been scathing in his evaluation of the primitive US radar stations on Oahu. Would Opie's criticisms have led to any improvement? Opie had watched the Med Fleet sail frequently all over the Mediterranean; he surely would have questioned the Monday through Friday operation of the Pacific Fleet. Would Admiral Kimmel have changed the schedule? The man who had shared whiskey and eggs at 3 AM with the debriefed pilots from *Illustrious*' Swordfish squadrons could have made a strong impression on the man responsible for tracking the Japanese aircraft carriers: his Naval Academy classmate "Eddie" Layton. Would Layton have remembered Opie's remarks when in late November, 1941 his department had lost track of those Japanese carriers, and Admiral Kimmel had teased him by saying, "You mean they might be rounding Diamond Head right now?"[28] Questions like these have no answer, though it is impossible to keep from asking them.

Epilogue

The United States Naval Institute was founded in 1873 to advance the study and discussion of naval matters. It is a private organization, a very early "think tank," but it has always had a very close relationship with the US Navy. The Institute has encouraged naval personnel of all ranks to write for Institute publications and submit photos and stories of sailors and the sea. As part of its program of encouragement, the Institute in the 1920's began running a Prize Essay Contest, inviting the submission of essays on naval matters, offering a cash prize and publication in the monthly *USNI Proceedings*. The 1937 Prize Essay contest offers a compellingly ironic conclusion to the story of the Taranto raid and its aftermath.

One of the essays submitted in the 1937 Prize Essay Contest was "Aerial Attacks on Fleets at Anchor" by Lt. Commander Logan C. Ramsey, USN[1]. In his essay, Ramsey spells out all of the advantages that aircraft would enjoy while attacking a fleet at anchor, and all of the disadvantages limiting such a fleet's ability to defend itself. In seven pages that show remarkable prescience, Ramsey makes the following points:

- A fleet must be at maximum readiness when at sea and liable to encounter a hostile fleet: hence, it must be at less than maximum readiness when at anchor.

- A fleet at anchor allows the enemy to choose the time of attack; including attacking at night, perhaps dropping flares for illumination of the target.

- An enemy's task of locating the target is much easier when that target is a "geographical position" rather than a "mobile objective."

- A fleet at anchor is less able to defend itself because it is unable to maneuver, it is not in a tactical formation allowing coordinated action, and its guns may be "masked by docks, buildings, or other ships."

- The ships of a fleet at anchor will not be fully manned, due to shore leave and the need for ships' personnel to attend to duties such as repair, refueling, and resupply.

- The appearance of attacking aircraft may be very sudden, so the defense must be "dynamic": searching for, finding, and attacking enemy aircraft carriers before they can launch their planes.

- The "traditional concept" of a fleet anchorage, with ship types berthed together, offers a "perfectly marvelous target for a squadron of hostile torpedo planes!" The low altitude at which such planes attack makes anti-aircraft gunnery - from both ship and shore - much more difficult.

- Torpedo nets and booms may be necessary to provide an adequate defense for such closely berthed targets.

- Large anchorages may require floating AA batteries - or a new form of AA ship - to adequately cover the area.

- An adequate search plan for an isolated naval base would require a 760 mile circle around the base to be flown by patrol aircraft each day before sunset.

All of this was set down on paper in late 1936; four years before the Taranto raid and at a time when naval aviation was far less capable than it would be when war broke out. In the information about authors that appeared at the back of the magazine, Ramsey noted that the idea for the essay came to him after hearing other officers opine that the development of air power would force fleets to retreat to safe harbors[2]. Said Ramsey, "Like others, I had assumed that once in port the hazard with respect to hostile air operations was over." Overcoming the limits of conventional wisdom was for Ramsey the beginning of a thought process that would lead him to an essay that was remarkably predictive of the course of events leading to December 7, 1941.

Ramsey's essay did not win the Prize Essay Contest. Judged by the order of publication, he ranked fourth out of the fourteen contest entries that were published. The winning essay was "Naval Limitations" by Lt. H. H. Smith-Hutton, USN[3]. It appeared in the April edition of

Proceedings. First Honorable Mention was awarded to "Naval Power as a Preserver of Neutrality and Peace" by Captain Dudley W. Knox, USN[4], which was published in May. "Naval Strategy in the Adriatic Sea During the World War" by Professor A. E. Sokol of Stanford University appeared in the August issue, 32 pages prior to Ramsey's essay[5]. From September to January, ten other Prize Essay submissions were published.

Despite his clear analysis and the remarkable accuracy of his forecasts, Ramsey ended his essay with two long paragraphs discussing the inaccurate and unclear opinions about air power held by "a large section of public opinion in the United States." He describes the common fear that in the event of war, "our cities and towns might be subjected to indiscriminate and widespread bombing or gas attacks by literally thousands of hostile planes." Although he discounts this idea, and provides a factual description of the true capabilities and numbers of "hostile aircraft" in existence at that time, he uses this discussion as a segue into his own opinions of a "transoceanic aerial raid." Such a raid, says Ramsey, would be extremely hazardous to the attacker - despite the earlier recitation of all the advantages held by aircraft attacking fleets at anchor and the disadvantages of the defenders - and, therefore, "would constitute a strategical blunder unexcelled by any in naval history." Having thus so convincingly laid out what might happen in the future if aircraft attacked a fleet at anchor, Ramsey lamely ends with "it can't happen here."

In such a conflict of sentiments, we find the beginning of all successful surprise attacks. After a disaster, the public always cries that this should have been foreseen and prevented, as it did after December 7th, and September 11th as well. Seeing the possibility of attack is often the individual inspiration of one person: like Ramsey, or the FBI agent who wondered about the frequency of young

Arab men taking flying lessons[6]. Granting little or no probability to the attack is more often a group activity, where commonly held notions are never challenged or examined[7]. Thus, real preparedness requires both the flash of insight from a brilliant individual and the healthy discussion and argument among a group. In 1940, Opie was prevented from adding the flash of brilliance or challenging the "it can't happen here" mentality of the Naval establishment in Hawaii by physical separation: he was not allowed to fly to Hawaii. Perhaps in future, electronic forms of contact may supercede the face to face kind. Secure "chat rooms" or blogs may allow security professionals to exchange ideas and provoke one another into new patterns of thought. A partial step in this direction may have already been taken: the government has created a new software product "called A-Space, a sort of Facebook for spies."[8] That might be the best way to insure that "it *doesn't* happen here."

One final irony puts an end to this story. As the Japanese planes zoomed low over American ships and airfields and bombs began to fall on that fateful Sunday morning, a naval officer at the Ford Island base picked up a microphone and broadcast an unforgettable message: "Air Raid, Pearl Harbor. This is not a drill." That officer's name was Logan C. Ramsey.

NOTES

The primary sources for this work are the reports filed by Opie and his successors with the Office of the Chief of Naval Operations and the Office of Naval Intelligence. These are found at the National Archives within Record Group 38. Grouped under the title, "Reports From Naval Attaches", the reports are briefly described on index cards, which have been transferred to microfilm for easier viewing. The Navy in 1940 used an arcane and difficult filing system involving a file categorization and a serial number. In the notes, I provide a specific file reference and serial number for most significant reports, such as Opie's Taranto report of 14 November, 1940(A-1-z/22863D).

Other valuable primary sources include Opie's Service Records and Evaluation Reports, the collected papers of a number of naval officers found at the Operational Archives of the Naval Historical Center at the Washington Navy Yard, and the Oral History Collection of the US Naval Institute.

The US Naval Institute maintains a library of oral histories which contains a number of interviews with naval officers who served as neutral observers in 1940 and 1941. In addition to any specifically cited below, those consulted for this study included: William R. Smedberg, Henri H. Smith-Hutton, Fitzhugh Lee, Odale D. Waters, Jr, Draper Kaufman, Donald McDonald, Bernard L. Austin, Ruthven Libby, James Fife, Jr., Ernest M. Eller, and Elliott B. Strauss.

There have been five good books about the Taranto raid: Newton & Hampshire, Schofield, Smithers, Lowry & Wellham, and Wragg. All are reliable on the battle and the events leading up to it, but only the first and last mention Opie, and only briefly. Wragg calls Opie "the ship's USN liaison officer", as if every RN vessel had one. None of these works reports on Opie's intelligence mission or his large volume of reporting on the war in the Mediterranean from August, 1940 through March, 1941.

Introduction

1. Acker, Commander F. C., "Taranto - 'ABC' Copenhagens the Enemy", *USNI Proceedings*, August, 1947, pp 907 - 912.

2. Dorwart, Jeffrey M., *Conflict of Duty*, Annapolis, Naval Institute Press, 1983, p 136.

The Raid

1. Schofield, p 16.

2. Opie, John N., "British Attack on Taranto on the Night of 11/12 November, 1940", National Archives, Record Group 38, File A-1-z, Registration 22863-D.

3. Tute, Warren, *The Deadly Stroke*, New York, Cowan McCann, & Geohagen, 1973.

4. Sadkovich, James J.(ed.), *Reevaluating Major Naval Combatants of World War II*, New York, Greenwood Press, 1990.

5. Angelucci, Enzo & Matricardi, Paolo, *World War II Airplanes*, Volumes I and II, Chicago, Rand McNally, 1978.

6. Rower, J. & Hummelchen, G., *Chronology of the War at Sea 1939-1945*, Annapolis, Naval Institute Press, 1992.

7. Report from Commander Ralph A. Oftsie, Naval Attache for Air, London, 19 August, 1941, forwarding "Air Attacks on Italian Harbors by Naval Aircraft", RN summary prepared for Admiral Lyster, dated 5 February, 1941. Found in National Archives, Record Group 38.

8. Wragg, pp 35 - 39.

9. Wragg, pp 67 - 74.

10. Wragg, p 82.

11. Rower & Hummelchen, *Chronology of the War at Sea*, pp 40-41; and Opie's Taranto Report.

12. Schofield, p 27, Newton & Hampshire, p 64, and Wragg, pp 86- 87.

13. Schofield, p 27.

14. Opie's Taranto Report, attached action report by *Illustrious'* Captain Denis Boyd, RN.

15. Bragadin, Marc Antonio, *The Italian Navy in WWII*, Annapolis, Nava Institute Press, 1957 p 44.

16. *Ibid.*, p 45.

17. Rower & Hummelchen, *p 41*.

18. Newton & Hampshire, p 92, and Lowry, Thomas P. and Wellham, John W. G., *The Attack on Taranto*, Mechanicsburg, PA, Stackpole Books, 1995, p 62.

19. Wragg, p 91.

20. Lamb DSO DSC RN, Charles, *To War in a Stringbag*, Garden City, NY, Nelson Doubleday, 1980, p 122. The wag was Lt. N. J. "Blood" Scarlett, RN.

21. Lowry & Wellham, p 91, and Opie Report, 11/4/40, National Archives, Record Group 38, R-6-a/20299.

22. Newton & Hampshire, p 97.

23. Maund, MR, in Winton, John(ed), *The War at Sea*, New York, Morrow, 1968, pp 86-87.

24. Sutton, A. W. F., "The Attack", *Air Pictorial*, October, 1967, p 344.

25. The details of each pilot's course and conduct come from Captain Denis Boyd's 12-page after action report, attached by Opie to his Taranto Report, National Archives, RG 38, A-1-z/22863-D.

26. Wragg, p 104; Opie's Taranto report.

27. Wragg, pp 119-120.

28. Schofield, p. 79.

29. Newton & Hampshire, p 165.

The Observer

1. Opie, John Newton, *A Rebel Cavalryman with Lee Stuart and Jackson*, W. B. Conkey Co, 1899, Press of Morningside Bookshop, 1972.

2. *The Lucky Bag*, 1924, US Naval Academy, p 259.

3. Opie's Service Record, obtained from The National Personnel Records Center, St Louis, MO.

4. "Report of Compliance With Orders", June 11, 1940, in Opie's Service Record.

5. Leutze, James R., "Technology and Bargaining in Anglo-American Naval Relations", USNI *Proceedings*, June, 1977, p 56.

6. "A Survey of Relationships with the Headquarters of the Special Naval Observer, London and the Commander, US Naval Forces in Europe during World War II", author not identified, found in the *Papers of Admiral Harold R. Stark*, Operational Archives, Naval Historical Center, Washington Navy Yard, Washington, DC, Box 27. On page 44, this source states that Opie was "sent over by the Bureau of Ships in June, 1940, solely to look into the question of minesweeping".

7. Opie's Report dated 7 August 1940, National Archives, RG 38, O-6-e/5675-A.

8. Opie's Report dated 1 July 1940, National Archives, RG 38, O-6-a/18415.

9. Opie's Report dated 29 August 1940, National Archives, RG 38, A-1-z/22863-D.

10. Opie's Reports dated 14 October, 1940(F-6-e/22874-B) and 4 November 1940(O-5-d/22598).

11. Opie's 5 October 1940 Report(F-6-e/22853-D).

12. Opie's 18 October 1940 Report(F-6-e/22853-D).

13. Opie's 19 October 1940 Report(F-6-e/22853-F).

14. Opie's 4 November 1940 Repport(O-5-d/22598).

15. Opies's 19 October, 4 November, and 14 November Reports (F-6-e/22853-G and F-6-e/22853-D).

16. Alan G. Kirk's Report from London dated 6 February 1041 which quotes Opie's 16 January 1941 letter to Kirk(F-6-e/22853-H).

17. Dorwart, Jeffrey, *Conflict of Duty*, Annapolis, Naval Institute Press, 1983, p 136.

18. Opie's 4 November 1940 Report(R-6-a/20299).

19. Opie's Taranto Report, dated 14 November 1940(A-1-z/22863-D).

20. Opie's Report dated 14 November 1940(F-6-e/22853-H).

21. Opie's 15 November 1940(O-6-c/5355-S).

22. Opie's 20 November 1940(E-12-c/20607-A).

23. Opie's 31 December 1940(F-6-e/22853-G).

24. Alan G. Kirk's 6 February 1941 Report quoting Opie's 16 January letter to Kirk(F-6-e/22853-H).

25. Opie's 6 March 1941 Report(F-6-e/22874-D).

26. Opie's 10 March 1941 Report(F-6-e/22853-I)

27. "Report of Compliance With Orders", 23 April 1941, from Opie's Service Record.

28. Opie's 29 April 1941 Report(F-6-e/22853-I).

29. Opie's Service Record.

30. Letter of Admonition, 30 January 1941, signed M. L. Deyo, Commander Destroyers, US Atlantic Fleet; and Deyo's letter of 11 February 1941 accepting report of investigation by Commander Valery Havard, USN, into the boiler damage aboard *USS Bache*. Found at the National Archives, Record Group 38.

31. Opie's Service Record.

32. Opie's Obituary, *San Diego Union*, 11 December, 1975, p A-19.

Aftermath

1. Schofield, pp 53-54, Wragg, pp 123-125, *New York Times*, November 14, 1940 pp 1 & 2.

2. Kincaid, Captain Thomas C., USN, Naval Attache Rome, Reports dated 11/14/1940 and 12/3/1941, Record Group 38, National Archives.

3. Rohwer & Hummelchen, p 107, Smithers, pp 135 - 137.

4. Wragg, pp 179 - 182. In his book, *Washington Goes to War*, David Brinkley told a story of a *femme fatale* British spy code-named "Cynthia" who seduced the Italian Naval Attache to Washington, DC, an officer named Alberto Lais, and obtained secret codes from him. Brinkley states that this information was used by the RN in the Taranto attack. There is some doubt about whether the story - told to Brinkley by Alan Dulles - is true: Lais' family successfully sued the original author of the tale. If it is true, it certainly related to Cape Matapan, not to Taranto.

5. Bragadin, pp 354 - 367, Sadkovich, pp 148 - 149.

6. Ansel, Walter, *Hitler and the Middle Sea*, Durham, NC, Duke University Press, 1972.

7. Ansel, Walter, Letter to the Editor, *USNI Proceedings*. February, 1960, pp 101 - 102, and *The Reminiscences of Rear Admiral Walter C. W. Ansel, USN(Retired)*, US Naval Institute, Annapolis, MD, 1972, pp 77 - 89.

8. *New York Times*, November 14, 1940, p 1.

9. Kimball, Warren F. (Editor), *Churchill and Roosevelt: The Complete Correspondence*, Princeton University Press, 1984, pp 83 - 85.

10. Smithers, pp 141 - 142.

11. Prange, Gordon W., *At Dawn We Slept*, New York, NY, McGraw Hill, 1981, p 14.

12. *Ibid.*, p 37.

13. *Ibid.*, p 40.

14. Ansel, Walter C., *Reminiscences...*, pp 77 - 79.

15. *Ibid.*, pp 87 - 89. The full text of the Knox letter is reproduced on pages 89a, 89b, and 89c.

16. Prange, p 16.

17. Ibid., pp 41 - 44.

18. *Papers of Admiral Harold R. Stark, USN*, Operational Archives, Naval Historical Center, Washington Navy Yard, Washington, DC.

19. *Ibid.*

20. *Ibid.*

21. Record Group 38, National Archives, A-1-z/22863F-J.

22. Stark *Papers*

23. Ansel, Walter C., "The Taranto Lesson", in *Air Raid: Pearl Harbor!*, Paul Stillwell (editor), Annapolis, MD, Naval Institute Press, 1981, p 74.

24. *The World at War*, Documentary Film, Thames Television, 1980, Episode 6.

25. Fioravanzo, Giuseppe, Vice Admiral, Italian Navy, "The Japanese Military Mission to Italy in 1941", *USNI Proceedings*, January, 1956, pp 24 - 32.

26. Stark *Papers*, and Prange, p 159.

27. Record Group 38, National Archives, A-1-z/22863F-J.

28. Prange, p 440.

Epilog

1. "Aerial Attacks on Fleets at Anchor", Lt. Commander Logan C. Ramsey, USN, *USNI Proceedings*, August, 1937, pp 1126 - 1132.

2. USNI Proceedings, August, 1937, p. 1216.

3. "Naval Limitations", Lieutenant Henry H. Smith-Hutton, USN, *USNI Proceedings*, April, 1937, pp 463 - 476.

4. "Naval Power as a Preserver of Neutrality and Peace", Captain Dudley W. Knox, USN(Ret), *USNI Proceedings*, May, 1937, pp 619 - 626.

5. "Naval Strategy in the Adriatic Sea During the World War", A. E. Sokol, *USNI Proceedings*, August, 1937, pp 1077 - 1092.

6. *The 911 Comission Report, Final Report of the National Commission on Terrorist Attacks Upon the United States*, New York, W. W. Norton & Company, 2004, p. 272.

7. Janis, Irving, *Victims of Groupthink*, Boston, Houghton-Mifflin, 1972.

8. See "A World of Connections" a Special Report contained in the January 30, 2010 edition of *The Economist*, pp 15 - 16.

Bibliography

Acker, F. C., "Taranto - "ABC" Copenhagens the Enemy", *USNI Proceedings*, 1947, pp 907-12.

Angelucci, Enzo, and Paolo Matricardi, *World War II Airplanes*, Vol 1 & 2, Chicago, Rand McNally, 1978.

Ansel, Walter C., *Hitler and the Middle Sea*, Durham, Duke University Press, 1972.

-----"Letter to the Editor", *USNI Proceedings*, March, 1959, p 101.

Baldwin, Hanson, "Britain's Fleet Strikes", New York Times, 14 November, 1940, p 8.

-----*The Crucial Years*: 1939-41, New York, Harper & Row, 1976.

-----*What the Citizen Should Know About the Navy*, New York, W. W. Norton, 1941.

Barmett, Corelli, *Engage the Enemy More Closely*, New York, W. W. Norton, 1991.

Bernotti, Romeo, "Italian Naval Policy Under Fascism", *USNI Proceedings*, July 1956, pp 722-731.

Bolt, A. S., "How the Tactics for the Raid Were Developed", *Air Pictorial*, 1967, pp 342-43.

Bragadin, Marc Antonio, *The Italian Navy in WWII*, Annapolis, Naval Institute Press, 1957.

Debelot, Raymond, *The Struggle for the Mediterranean*, Princeton, Princeton University Press, 1951.

Dorwart, Jeffery, *Conflict of Duty*, Annapolis, Naval Institute Press, 1983.

Fioravanzo, Giusepppe, "The Japanese Miltary Mission to Italy", *USNI Proceedings*, January, 1956, pp 24-32.
-----"Italian Strategy in the Mediterranean", *USNI Proceedings*, September, 1958, pp 65-72.

Gibson, Hugh, ed., *The Ciano Diaries*, Garden City, NY, Doubleday, 1946.

Gleason, S. E., and William L. Langer, *The Undeclared War*, Gloucester, MA, Peter Smith, 1953.

Gunther, Rohwer, and G. Hummelchen, *Chronology of the War at Sea*, London, Ian Allen, 1972.

Hampshire, A. C., "Triumph at Taranto", *USNI Proceedings*, March, 1959, pp 71-79.

Heinrichs, Waldo, *Threshold of War*, New York, Oxford University Press, 1988.

Howard, Michael, *The Mediterranean Strategy in WWII*, New York, Praeger, 1968.

Janis, Irving, *Victims of Groupthink*, Boston, Houghton-Mifflin, 1972.

Kimball, Warren F., ed., *Churchill and Roosevelt: The Complete Correspondence*, Princeton, Princeton University Press, 1984.

Kimmel, Husband E., *Admiral Kimmel's Story*, Chicago, Henry Regnery, 1955.

Knox, Dudley W., "Naval Power as a Preserver of Neutrality and Peace", *USNI Proceedings*, May, 1937, pp 619-626.

Lamb, Charles, *To War in a Stringbag*, Garden City, NY, Nelson Doubleday, 1980.

Leutze, James R., *Bargaining for Supremacy*, Chapel Hill, University of North Carolina Press, 1977.

----- "Technology and Bargaining in Anglo-American Naval Relations", *USNI Proceedings*, June, 1977, pp 50-61.

Levite, Ariel, *Intelligence and Strategic Surprises*, New York, Columbia University Press, 1987.

Lewin, Ronald, *Ultra Goes to War*, London, Hutchinson, 1978.

Lowry, Thomas P., and John W. G. Wellham, *The Attack on Taranto*, Mechanicsburg, PA, Stackpole Books, 1995.

Maugeri, Franco, *From the Ashes of Disgrace*, New York, Reynal & Hitchcock, 1948.

Newton, Donald, and A. C. Hampshire, *Taranto*, London, W. Kimber, 1959.

Playfair, I. S. O., et al, *The Mediterranean and the Middle East*, London, HMSO, 1954.

Porch, Douglas, *The Path to Victory: The Mediterranean Theater in WWII*, New York, Farrar, Straus, and Giroux, 2004.

Potter, John D., *Yamamoto: The Man Who Menaced America*, New York, Viking Press, 1956.

Prange, Gordon W., and Donald M. Goldstein and Katherine V. Dillon, *At Dawn We Slept*, New York, McGraw Hill, 1981.

Ramsey, Logan C., "Aerial Attacks on Fleets At Anchor", *USNI Proceedings*, August, 1937, pp 1126-1132.

Richardson, J. O., *On the Treadmill to Pearl Harbor*, Washington, DC, Naval History Division, Department of the Navy, 1973.

Roskill, Steven, *White Ensign: The British Navy at War*, Annapolis, Naval Institute Press, 1973.

Schofield, B. B., *The Attack on Taranto*, Annapolis, Naval Institute Press, 1973.

Smith-Hutton, H. H., "Naval Limitations", *USNI Proceedings*, April, 1937, pp 463-476, (1937 Prize Essay)

Smith, Dennis Mack, *Mussolini*, New York, Knopf, 1982.

Smithers, A. J., *Taranto 1940*, Annapolis, Naval Institute Press, 1995.

Stillwell, Paul, *Air Raid: Pearl Harbor!*, Annapolis, Naval Institute Press, 1981.

Sutton, A. W. F., "The Attack", *Air Pictorial*, 1967, 343-345.

Thames Television, *The World at War*, Chapter 6: Banzai, Interviews with Genda Minoru and Fuchida Mitsuo.

Thetford, Owen, *Aircraft of the RAF 1918 - 1957*, London, Pulman & Co., 1957.

Tute, Warren, *The Deadly Stroke*, New York, Coward, McCann & Geohegen, 1973.

Wheeler, Gerald E., *Kincaid of the Seventh Fleet*, Washington, DC, Naval Historical Center, Department of the Navy, 1995.

Winton, John, ed., *The War At Sea*, New York, Morrow, 1968.

Woodhouse, Henry, "Torpedo Planes in WWII", *USNI Proceedings*, 1941, pp 1750-56.

Wragg, David, *Swordfish*, London, Weidenfield & Nicholson, 2003.